WALKING
THROUGH
DARKNESS

WALKING THROUGH DARKNESS

A Nature-Based Path
to Navigating Suffering and Loss

By SANDRA INGERMAN and LLYN ROBERTS

STERLING ETHOS
New York

STERLING ETHOS
New York

STERLING ETHOS and the distinctive Sterling Ethos logo
are registered trademarks of Sterling Publishing Co., Inc.

Text © 2023 Sandra Ingerman and Llyn Roberts

Interior art © 2023 Eben Herrick

ISBN 978-1-4549-5085-1
ISBN 978-1-4549-5086-8 (e-book)

Library of Congress Control Number: 2023934267

For information about custom editions, special sales, and premium purchases,
please contact specialsales@unionsquareandco.com.

Printed in Canada

2 4 6 8 10 9 7 5 3 1

unionsquareandco.com

Cover design by Jo Obarowski
Cover image by Robsonphoto/Shutterstock.com
Interior design by Kevin Ullrich

We dedicate this book to the brave souls
who walk through the darkness and into a life
filled with beauty and magic . . .

And to Nature. We share honor, love,
kindness, and respect with all in the web of life
with whom we share this beautiful Earth.

CONTENTS

Introduction

Sandra

There comes a time in everyone's life when we go through a period where loss and tragedy bring us into the darkness. We enter territory where we feel lost, devoid of tools, and directionless, with no way to know how to move or where to take our next step. In many spiritual and psychological traditions, this time can be called the Dark Night of the Soul. In this book, I am referring to how the Dark Night of the Soul is experienced in the practice of shamanism.

This is not to be confused with psychological literature that talks about the Dark Night of the Soul. In this book, I am referring to the Dark Night of the Soul as a time of initiation where life brings us to a place of loss. It leads to us softening our ego, letting go of judgments, reaching higher states of consciousness, and changing our values. When we return to a full life after an initiation, we have more tools and spiritual strength to share in our community. But first our ego needs polishing to help chip away at our hard spots, open our closed hearts, and strengthen our spirits to carry us through all kinds of dark nights.

Our periods of deep suffering are important times in our lives. Yes, these are times of pain, but they also represent great growth and transformation. They are initiations that transform us into new people with a new desire to change and live a more balanced and healthy life. The losses we experience soften us and help to relieve the burdens of our past.

We would have hoped to have received a road map and tools from our elders. And some of us did. But for some, very little knowledge or training was passed down from previous generations. Most of the information on how to follow the path when the darkness descends on us has been lost. Throughout history, that has been one of the roles of grandparents, aunts, and uncles: to tell the stories that teach us how to get through suffering and how to get our lives back from pain while standing strong in our true power. We don't tell those stories to children anymore. And they are so necessary. We need those stories!

I have had tough shamanic initiations throughout my life. Although I grew up in Brooklyn without any special training, from a young age I was naturally in touch with the spiritual forces around me, and I was blessed with a strong connection with Nature.

My life has been filled with one shamanic initiation after another: near-death experiences, illnesses, my suicidal ideation. I was hit by lightning at the age of seven. Before that, I had a life-threatening case of the measles and had to be kept in complete darkness for a time—a practice that is a common shamanic initiation. I drowned in Mazatlán at the age of nineteen. When I was twenty-five, I drove my car off a cliff when a huge blast of dust from the car in front of me blinded my vision. This event could have killed me and the other passengers in the car, but we were divinely protected and none of us got hurt. However, we all had the classic symptoms of a near-death experience … And if that was not enough, at age twenty-eight, a boulder careened off Mount Shasta and headed straight at me. I dropped to the ground, and the boulder missed me by five feet according to observers.

A priest I trusted told me I was called too early. My life has been a series of initiations, one after another, with only the support of my inner spirit and Nature. Even today, the initiations continue to break down my shell, teaching me about the power of love and how to tap into my full spiritual strength, which is the only way to survive during such trials.

In 2015, when I was sixty-two, a sudden moment changed my life. I was teaching a teleconferencing course, and when I hung up, I felt very strange. I felt like I was hit by lightning and had to hold on to the wall to keep myself from passing out. I drank some tea and went to bed. In the morning, I woke up to the fact that I had developed a very rare and mysterious brain disorder. It is a movement disorder that is not progressive, but at the same time it took away a lot of my ability to function in life.

I never had elders to guide me through my initiations. I only knew what to do from my shamanic studies, which told me that an initiate must find their inner spiritual strength to get through on their own. And I did!

But in these times, without any elders guiding me and having my back, I felt like I had been dropped out of an airplane in the middle of the night with no flashlight, food, map, anything for comfort or direction. I just felt lost.

I was determined to develop a road map using the tools I found to help me through all my life challenges.

How did I find ways to travel through the darkness? What about my times of hopelessness? How did I transform that state? How did I learn to determine that there are tricksters who will tell you they can help but lead you off the path of healing and rebirth? And how did I learn that it is important to always take little steps forward and not sit down in the dark?

In our culture, we tend to focus on positive thinking and always on our greatest dreams. But from a shamanic and nature-based point of view, there is sculpting of our ego that needs to be done. Consider the waves that run through the Grand Canyon and how, through many eons, they carved out such a beautiful change.

In this book, I am excited to join with Llyn Roberts. As we did in our previous work, *Speaking with Nature*, we have chosen certain animals, plants, trees, insects, and other beings in nature to provide metaphorical guidance as we walk the path through suffering to renewal and change. Nature can be a guide and healer. Nature is healing balm.

Llyn and I, both elders, have been very successful in teaching shamanism and helping people learn how to find their way through the darkness. In this book, we offer the immense knowledge we have gained both through our studies and our life challenges, and we offer a path to finding meaning in difficult times. There is always a way forward and through when guided by our own spiritual light, strength, and power.

In shamanic cultures, it was only the initiates who survived who were welcomed back into the community. By adding to the community the knowledge they had gained from their experiences, it could continue to thrive. I invite you to really work with the material in this book in order to share with and inspire others in your community.

The Dark Night of the Soul is the portal into living in a different dimension of life. My reason for writing this book is not to tell my story; it is to give those who are struggling the benefit of what I have learned so they will be able to apply it to their own lives.

There are endless books and courses on how to stay positive, but this book is about the beneficial aspects of darkness. Darkness is filled with exquisite teachings for the brave souls who are willing to let go and travel to the depths of our inner world to see what states of consciousness and ways of behaving need to be removed, transformed, accepted, acknowledged, or discreated.

It was such a joy and honor to work with Llyn while we wrote *Speaking with Nature*. We had such a unique way of working and honoring each other's process. Llyn is an amazing writer, and I am in awe of her abilities to work with metaphorical stories and teachings. We really came together again to write this book, allowing ourselves to show our vulnerabilities while also celebrating our spiritual strength and focusing on what was truly needed to cope with challenges.

While writing *Speaking with Nature*, Llyn and I decided to use circular storytelling versus linear essays. This is a feminine approach and an old-time way of sharing wisdom that feeds our souls. We are all full of information. Our essays show readers how to live what we have learned.

During these times, we can do more than survive. We can thrive.

We offer these lessons in finding your intuition so that you can move forward, no matter what challenges you face.

Llyn

We've all known difficult life passages, and anyone who is sensitive feels the immense suffering and fragmentation in the world. It's impossible to ignore the challenges that nature and humans face now.

I have been working with ancient cultures since the age of twenty-five. Many of these cultures hold prophecies about our current times of upheaval. The South American "Eagle and the Condor" prophecy foretells the era in which we are living as one of peril yet also great opportunity. How we know ourselves can change. Living in harmony with the Earth, integrating our hearts with our minds, and blending the spiritual qualities of life with the material can reshape our reality. The Andean Quechua people call this current period "Pachacuti," which means "transformer of the worlds."

Although the idea of living in an era foreseen by ancient peoples as one that can transform us is auspicious and amazing, the experience of it is humbling. There is chaos, suffering, tragedy, and death. The path we all walk together through this initiatory gauntlet may take from us all that we hold dear. Life is precious and tender now, more than ever.

I am no stranger to challenge.

Half of my ancestry is Celtic, and the other half is French Canadian. I grew up in a working-class ethnic enclave in New Hampshire known as Frenchtown. My family did not have much money, and my beautiful and creative mother, who lost her own childhood to parental alcoholism and poverty, gave birth to me when she was just seventeen. My mother was emotionally unstable, which made our home life troubled. My sorrow was lifted when I lay on the grass to gaze at the sky, skated on rivers and ponds, played in muddy creek beds, and whispered to snow-dusted trees. Being in nature healed and soothed me. I was also helped by spirit presences both felt and heard.

Like Sandra, I have had brushes with death. When I was five, my three-year-old brother and I were lifted from our beds in the middle of the night by my dad and our upstairs neighbor when the small kitchen adjacent to our tiny, shared bedroom caught fire. The men threw blankets over our heads and carried us through an inferno to save our lives. The day before my fifty-second birthday, I nearly bled to death. I have known anxiety, depression, relationship hardships, and many other trials. After my son and I survived his precarious birth, my health grew fragile, and for years I endured a spiritual emergency, sometimes fighting for my sanity. This terrifying time compelled me to work with diverse indigenous shamanic peoples, some in remote areas, who saw my illness as an induction by spirit.

I know I am not alone in facing life's hardships and losses. And although my life hasn't been easy, each trial has had its gifts, which have sometimes taken me years to fully realize. The journey ultimately strengthened and deepened me.

The shamanic path is fraught with many tests. Likewise, within shamanic ceremony, traditional people expressed not only joy but grief, anger, death, fear, loss, and chaos through their movements, sounds, and rituals. All of life's rhythms were embodied, witnessed, and integrated—not constrained by judgment or even by language.

Beyond shamanism, cultures the world over are steeped in story and myths that offer road maps for the "descent" into darkness. These acknowledge how hard life can be. They remind us of nature's rhythms of gestation, hibernation, death, and destruction.

Within ancient traditions, as in nature, death is always followed by rebirth, renewal, and regeneration.

Life's hurdles can strip us of the false ideas that we hold. As old notions of ourselves and our world die, we can take truer, and often surprisingly new, pathways.

As Sandra and I were putting the final touches on our previous book, *Speaking with Nature*, nature beings came to me in dreams as teachers. These allies helped me nourish my highly sensitive nature in the middle of a complex world. They guided me to forgotten inner places of love and creativity that my wounds concealed. I introduced working with these forces to my second-year apprentices. They experienced a deep sense of belonging with nature and a stronger bond with their soul. In being guided through their own obstacles and welcoming vulnerability, they became more genuine healers and teachers.

Nature-based spiritual traditions tell us we must seek the light in the dark. Maya elders taught that you could not have light without darkness. Druidic and other ancient systems instructed their initiates to retreat to the densest part of the forest or to the barren reaches of the desert to find their inner light.

As Sandra mentions, the part of modern spiritual culture that focuses primarily on positivity alone, casting darkness as bad, separates us from all of who we are—from our soul force and from the Earth. The dark that we perceive as bad is often a projection of the places within us—individually as well as culturally—that we have a hard time accepting. True power comes from embracing ourselves fully. As we do so, our outer reality may reflect less destructive extremes.

As we integrate more of the dark, it shines as richness. This wisdom is an age-old alchemy promising to forge us as fully human.

Though we may feel overwhelmed, lost, fearful, or angry as we grapple with uncertainty, every experience holds a treasure of spiritual light.

Allies from nature can guide us to the light, helping us touch what repels us and transform what makes us afraid. They also serve to remind us of archetypal, mythic, and creative forces that interweave throughout mundane life yet are so often neglected and denied. These include our innate intuition, as well as personal and collective healing opportunities our sorrows and illnesses can initiate.

Likewise, we can awaken to the intelligent force of our Earth Mother and the spirited forces in the land, water, winds, and cosmos. Nature's dark and shaded places, its liminal times, are extremely rich. Beautiful, magical life can grow there. The denial of Earth-honoring ways cuts us off from the fertile, powerful places hidden within nature—and within us.

Some nature beings Sandra and I present are threatened. As you read, you may find some qualities of endangered animals and ecosystems reflect aspects of humanity that are minimized, suppressed, abused, or forsaken.

The animals, luminary bodies, landscapes, and myriad aspects of nature in this book, as well as others that call to you, invite you to explore and deepen your relationship to their energies. Their stories, like myths and legends from ancient times, illuminate dark pathways we must all walk for humanity's wholeness to shine. Some beings are nocturnal, offering us vision in the dark, reminding us of the gift of being vulnerable and accepting guidance. They tell us that spirit and nature are with us in the darkest of times, even when we don't feel this to be true.

There is a lot of suffering and grief in the world now. Part of humanity's sadness comes from feeling separate from nature. With ecological changes and species destruction, many people fear that the Earth herself is dying. These events are heartbreaking, tragic. Yet, our sentient Planet Earth is an amazing, intelligent being. She knows how to renew herself, and so do we.

The essays in this book invite nature to help you cultivate strength, meaning, and beauty through the changes and challenges we face. We are one with the Earth, and she is here to love and to guide us. Let us also remember to give back to her all that we can.

CHAPTER 1

Coyote

Sandra

The day felt so still, like something was stirring in the energy fields. I had been having a really hard time with my life. Once again, I had said "yes" to too many work commitments, and my body was starting to rebel as if it were a coworker saying, "We cannot go on like this." I sensed a familiar feeling, a darkness getting ready to descend. Throughout my life, I have found that when my life journey brings me to a challenging place, I feel a stillness descend over me. It is as if a choice were being made. But by whom? Is it the universe or my own soul? And does it really matter? We are all on a journey, one that flows with the river of life and, of course, we can't always control the direction or the quality of this flow.

It felt like the universe heard my soul calling that it was time to dive deep into the Dark Night of the Soul. And the universe in return called in helping spirits to aid in creating the initiatory journey.

I felt like I was being thrown off a cliff, down into a deep, dark hole, where a territory brimming with lessons, healings, growth, and future evolutionary changes was occurring. In times like these, loved ones can only look from afar.

It was a test. It was a test to see whether I had the spiritual strength to face my own inner demons so that I could free myself from them and then learn how to live a life from my spiritual strength rather than being led around by my ego. It was a test and mine alone to face.

Loved ones and friends could light candles for me and cheer me on from afar. Candles are an important part of ceremonial work, as they hold sacred holy space during the ceremony, whether the ceremony spans an hour, a night, days, or weeks.

People could place prayer ties at sacred places, asking for protection for me. During this deep, dark journey, I would be sculpted into who I came here to be so that I could contribute to my community and live a meaningful and fulfilling life. Even the helping spirits and divine beings that I had come to trust and depend on took a step back on behalf of my next stage of growth.

When I felt myself descending into a dark time of life, I knew that guardian spirits would fill the hole that connects the Under World and the Outside World. In this space, noise is gone. The cacophony of living is gone. Although this space can be frightening, when I entered it, I knew that I was in a place where I could listen to the messages coming from deep within, shaping the next part of my life.

I knew what this stillness meant. For me, the world had become so noisy that I found myself needing to go down into the darkness and close the door to the outside world. It was so still. But at the same time, it was so dark: no tools, no signs, no compass, no direction. Just me, in that familiar place of knowing that soon my life would be dismembered once again so that I would be able to reach into the depths of my own soul. I would be in pain, but I would also change and evolve, like all living beings in nature do. Life is anything but stagnant. Even the darkness was filled with movement, even as I felt so static, stark, and lost in my new surroundings.

I began my adventure in this stark landscape knowing that during my journey I would meet many teachers in the form of nature beings. As I shared in the introduction, I have journeyed through the Dark Night of the Soul many times in my life. And there are both dangers and beauty when one lets the unknown take them into landscapes as dark as the sun is bright.

In the past, I had learned that one of the dangers of the darkness is that we have to have our intuition intact and know how to wield it with speed in the midst of trickster energy. There are forces always trying to lure us into a favorable position to be manipulated, and if we allow this to happen, we pay a huge price in the end.

After finding myself in this shadowy place, I did not waste time. I immediately brushed the cool earth off my pants and began my journey. But my first question was, Where would my journey lead? I felt like I had been dropped from an airplane at thirty thousand feet with a blindfold on my eyes and with no compass, flashlight, or road map.

I began my journey in the forest in what seemed like the dead of the night. I knew I had to walk for quite a while in order to get my bearings and shed the looping mental chatter I brought with me. I imagined my thoughts dropping away from me, like dead leaves returning to the ground in fall to create nurturance for the earth and for new growth.

I knew from previous vision quests that there were a lot of surprises. There were the beings who would see my weakness, wanting to take advantage of me. There would also be nature being allies reaching out to me seemingly from nowhere, offering some kindness or help.

But first, I knew I had to face one of the most dangerous beings on my quest: the trickster. It did not take me long to see bright yellow eyes staring at me in the distance. I knew I was already being stalked.

Coyotes walk the land of night, solo or in packs, looking for the weak to prey on. They are creatures who are highly intelligent and tuned in to their senses so they can run through the pinyon pine and juniper trees to find safety or to attack their prey.

Coyote is a powerful archetype to learn about while walking through the darkness. When we are weak and not tuned to our intuition, we can feel desperate for help. This leaves us open and vulnerable to seeing all help as necessary instead of understanding that there are people waiting to take advantage of the weak, those persons who are not grounded and are open to manipulation.

Coyote likes to walk with me for a while through the darkness. He gets close to me as if he is my friend. He is not threatening, but he has a wild look in his eyes. What does that wildness mean? What is he going to ask of me? He seems to have a grace and poise about him, but he seems too hungry. My intuition throws up a red flag, and I feel fear rise in my belly. This is a familiar sense I get when I meet a trickster. My body is telling me that it is time for me to set my boundaries and follow what my intuition is telling me.

Once we can stand strong in our intuition, we can enter the flow of the river of life knowing that we will always have our internal guidance to steer us away from the dark creatures that are waiting to take advantage of us, like Coyote.

However, these tricksters can make us question our intuition. We do have an innate, intuitive knowledge of what is right for us when it comes to healing, and energy like Coyote's can cause us to turn away from what will benefit us.

As we walk through the darkness, whom do we trust and whom do we stay away from? What are our spiritual, mental, and emotional tools? We need to explore, going through some very intense emotions, to release all the layers of thought and feeling preventing us from moving through our doubts and entering that portal into another dimension, where we perceive light and love instead of focusing on the denser energies of our own suffering. You are dying to yourself in this lifetime, so your true identity can shine through. The trials we go through are opportunities to push ourselves through the realms where tricksters beckon us off the path that would lead us to experiences of beauty, joy, and true connection with ourselves, others, our community, and all of nature.

We will learn how we are constantly fed with love during our journeys through the dark. Although we may not feel it, it is strengthening our spirits and carrying us through.

To find love and get to this place, we must first learn about the trickster energy that threatens us. When we feel lost, small, and insignificant, we become desperate. We end up trusting and being grateful for any being that shows up, saying they are here to offer help.

As I have shared before, my experiences have helped me to develop a compass I can easily use when I enter this territory of transformation. By reaching for this inner strength, I feel confident moving through death and confusion and into rebirth, illumination, and being reshaped into a higher being. But this was not an easy process.

One of my entries into the Dark Night of the Soul has been in recent years. I have developed a very mysterious and rare disorder. I was so desperate for help that I went everywhere searching for healing.

During this period, I ran into people who reminded me of coyotes, with their glaring, indecipherable eyes. Those who follow coyotes typically never return.

For me, Coyote manifested in the form of helpers who jumped out of nowhere, almost like they had materialized from the ethers, with promises of easy solutions. These people were just like a pack of Coyotes that I had felt my self being surrounded by so many times before.

But Coyote is not simply a predator. She has a wisdom side to her energy, which can so often be malevolent. Although these supposed "helpers" attempted to surround and devour me, it was Coyote who taught me how to turn this energy back on my tricksters. Coyote taught me how to stalk them, watching them closely through her eyes, eyes that could take in every nuance of movement and sound.

I had to start to work with the wisdom of Coyote, as I felt myself being consumed by trickster energy, and I needed Coyote's radar-like skills of observation to help me steer clear of those people who might have been well intentioned but in the end drove me further from who I really needed to be.

When we get desperate, we start to reach out for any place or person we think can offer us some help to alleviate our suffering. This can lead us into confusion, so we must use our intuition to guide ourselves. While Coyote energy can provide insight that will help you determine what you truly need, there are also those Coyote tricksters that will lead you in the wrong direction. But how do you distinguish them from those who will lead you in the right direction, where healing and guidance can happen?

As I have shared, in the territory of the Dark Night of the Soul, there are no flashlights, ropes, compasses, or maps to guide you. However, in these shadows, there are spiritual allies who will show themselves to you if you develop your intuition.

The tool of tapping into our intuition is so important in the world we are living in. As I wrote this book, a pandemic was impacting the lives of humans all over the world, wars raged, and the planet was subjected to acts of violence and devastating climatic changes. It can be difficult to maintain a connection to your own intuition if you feel dwarfed by the massive challenges of the world, which can make us feel so insignificant. When I can turn within to my divine spirit, filled with radiant light, I don't feel so small and powerless.

That is the reason why coyotes hunt in packs: to have more support. I truly feel that the times we are living in are leading us to find smaller communities, where we can live and be supported and support others in return. The world has just become too big. And we must look through the eyes of nature beings, such as a coyote, to learn the power of community and finding our territory—the land we call home.

Human beings are more divided than ever before. However, the spirit allies of the natural world, which we will meet and explore throughout this book, are united: they understand the need for strong connections. Coyote energy is solid. Coyotes have a knowing that they must form a strong community, with no weak links, or they will not be successful in their survival. When I found myself in a place where I did not know what news story to trust, what doctors to trust, what politicians to trust, and the list goes on ... I had to rely on my own internal knowing. Our divine spirit reflects the Creator, and we were born with every seed of knowledge within us just waiting to bloom in the right conditions.

In these times, the trap that a Coyote could lay is one that shakes our inner trust, and this is the most dangerous state in which we can enter the darkness. To avoid this kind of danger, we must find the right allies to help us. There are so many tricksters. When we develop the skills to recognize them, it's obvious that they're everywhere: in ads, in the news, and in our lives. Sometimes, if we look closely, we can even see their faces and eyes shape-shift so that they look like a Coyote.

I don't want to give coyotes a bad rap. After all, they are sentient beings, doing what they were taught to survive in life. Once there was a coyote who lived in the arroyo outside my house where I walked daily. This coyote was kind and gentle. I called him the "Mysterious Creature." He would walk with me but not stalk me. It was like he needed the company. Again, this is why it's so important to learn to differentiate various kinds of trickster energy—the kind that can be wise and instructive, and the kind that can hurt us. The universe itself can even possess a trickster energy, which can manifest in ways both positive and negative. When we are struggling, this kind of energy often manifests. Sometimes when we are struggling, the universe will trick us into putting the right person in our lives.

An example of this happened to me out of the blue. I received a letter from a man in his eighties who lived in another country. He was obviously a mystic. I don't know why he wrote me his letter. I wrote him back and gave him my email address. I told him that I would love to be in contact with him as he seemed like such an interesting man. He was a poet, and he sent me a book of poetry. Without me knowing it, although I think he knew it, he was tuned in to me.

With this poetry, he walked with me through part of my journey in the Dark Night of the Soul, telling me stories about the healing power of nature, which of course I knew; but because he was a poet, he told me these stories as a poet would tell them. He told me about his day and the beautiful beings he met. His words kept me moving forward on my arduous journey. Even though he didn't know the circumstances going on in my life, he became an amazing ally for me. I was just incredibly grateful. I learned that sometimes there's a trickster energy that enters your life not to harm or mislead you but to walk with you and keep you company while you find your own path through the darkness.

It really does get tricky, because while we should remain open to these kinds of unexpected allies, we also must learn to recognize red flags when they come up. When we access our intuition, we must go beyond what our ego tells us, because our ego attaches to what is being shared. We hear, "I know the cure for whatever illness you are dealing with." "You can trust me." "I know the real conspiracy theories going on right now." And so on. These are some examples of statements that throw people into dysregulation and chaos. Trickster energy seems to be alive all over the world, and just like in the animal kingdom, a being like Coyote leads his prey to its death.

The mind takes in all the false information when it is desperate. "Yes, I need to sign up for this." "Yes, I need that pill." "Yes, I need this podcast, this news story, this book, more courses."

The ego is reaching for help while the body holds the truth. With our body, we have our feeling sense. We feel textures in the world. But we also have our psychic sense, our clairsentience. And our body reacts with this sense when we hear a lie. We get an uncomfortable feeling in our body and have a sense something is not right. You might feel your body recoil. Or you might be more visual and perceive a literal red flag when someone is being a trickster. Some people have a very acute psychic sense of clairaudience and hear messages. So, you might hear your body telling you to get away from this person because they are not being truthful.

There is so much to be aware of. With so much noise, chaos, and false information, life can seem overwhelming. By getting your psychic senses stronger, you will encounter your own internal compass of who to come to and who to move away from.

Our intuition is our greatest ally in the Dark Night of the Soul. Our intuition gives us the compass that points to where to walk and teaches us how to watch for signs indicating when we'll need to walk right, left, or straight ahead. You don't meet demons in the Dark Night of the Soul, although some might. The only demon you meet is yourself. The tricksters you meet on your journey are people coming into your life who see that you are vulnerable.

Sometimes it is difficult to know when to move away from or closer to someone offering help. Some people need to be given a chance, like the lovely man who accompanied me for a while on my journey through darkness. Rather than a trickster who kept me sitting in the dark, he was an ally who helped me muster the strength to keep walking. He was put in my path by the universe to give me a gift, a blessing, and some tools for my journey. He walked with me in times when I truly felt I could not take another step.

This trickster energy is vital, but we must learn how to discern it even in times of struggle. It can keep us moving forward in dark times, when it is so important not to sit down and become paralyzed but rather to keep moving forward, like the river of life that keeps flowing home to Source.

Practice

Reflect on the trickster energy that might have entered your life, shifting you away from your destiny, your direction, and your own healing. This could be a trickster in your past or present.

Start by imagining you are going inside yourself so that you can hear your psychic senses speaking to you in the silence. You want to come up with a feeling, sound, or image when your intuition is truly engaged.

What is your body like when you *know* the truth? Do you see any red flags? Do you hear a message coming from deep within? Drop into your body and really tune in to what you are feeling, because your body always knows the truth.

Once you identify the signs that let you know whether you are with trickster energy or with an ally, you will be able to walk your path protected by your higher spirit and soul, which has all the knowledge within to live a life of joy and good health.

When you see the radiant eyes of Coyote watching you, is Coyote stalking you or wanting to walk with you as an ally? In the end, all nature beings can become allies through the lessons they have to teach us. And Coyote inspires us to reach into our soul and engage our intuition so we can be protected in life.

CHAPTER 2

Tundra Reindeer

Llyn

> Imagine a vast, treeless landscape that becomes lost in darkness through the long winter months. See in your mind's eye the lush cover of ground plants and wildflowers that blossom during the brief summer thaw on these otherwise barren lands.

Tundra reindeer live above the northern tree line in Arctic regions that are desolate to the visitor's eye. Many are herded by Eurasian nomadic peoples who rely on the animal for everything they need, including pulling their wooden sleighs. Semiwild reindeer herds travel hundreds of miles a year. With their herders, they migrate several times a week, only settling in one place for the wintriest months. Some tundra reindeer herds still roam free, including in North America, where they are called caribou.

Shamanic peoples of the far north have since time immemorial ridden the Reindeer spirit in shamanic trance and journey states to retrieve wisdom, power, and energy from other worlds to help individuals and their communities in this ordinary reality. Some say this is the origin of the myth of Santa Claus, who flies a reindeer-pulled sleigh filled with gifts from a magical place in the far north to brighten the heart and lighten the long, dark nights of winter.

Just as sparkling snowflakes and flying reindeer make us look up at the sky in wonder on cold moonless nights, when life grows ominous, the energy of Tundra Reindeer can make it a valuable ally, opening us to magic and possibility.

I experienced tundra reindeer, the reindeer people of the Nenets indigenous group, and the richness of tundra spaces when I traveled to the Yamal Peninsula in northwest Siberia in 2018. After flying west from Moscow, I sat in an all-terrain vehicle for a nine-hour drive into the tundra. The land yawned out in every direction.

Our Muscovite guide said he preferred the forest to the Arctic tundra, which to him was "nothing" as far as the eye could see. Our indigenous Nenets driver felt differently. He had lived on the tundra until age five, when he was taken from his family to live at a boarding school for most of each year. Being parted from his loved ones, their language and nomadic way of life still haunted this man. Through tears, he said the ancient ways of the reindeer people and the spirits of these lands made him feel alive.

Tundra land has little rainfall or soil nutrients to support animal or plant life. Other than the seasonal burst of flowers, only simple ground plants can survive the brutal weather, such as shrubs, grasses, and lichen. Although sturdy against cold, snow, and wind, tundra growth is highly sensitive to pollution, and if the soil is damaged, the plants may not grow back.

Veering off rugged truck tracks onto virgin ground, our driver stopped to deflate the massive Trekol tires to protect the tender lands.

After a long, bumpy drive, we spotted a *chum* (a teepee-like structure covered by reindeer skin). We parked a distance away, and I jumped out from the high truck cab. As soon as my feet hit the boggy earth, the wind almost knocked me over. I watched as white clouds raced across the sky. The howl was ceaseless. Rumbles soon joined the screaming winds. Huge lightning bolts lit up thunderclouds over the distant mountains. The air was electric.

The Nenets family bedded my two colleagues and me down that night on thick reindeer hides behind a flowered curtain on one end of the chum. The family of five nestled together on the other side. Their small herding dog lay inside, next to the entry flap. Drowsy from traveling and the heat from the woodstove, I fell fast asleep.

I woke up in the middle of the night hearing laughing, hollering, and footsteps outside as people ran around the chum. Children squealed. The dog yapped, and I wondered why the family hadn't let him out to run around with them. I listened to the happy ruckus for a long time until falling back to sleep.

The next morning, my colleague Ken Cervantes said he was awakened by the same sounds. I asked our guide, who had slept soundly, to please ask the family about what Ken and I heard. Could we join them outside tonight?

I nodded knowingly to the Nenets husband and wife as our guide spoke my message. Their blank looks confused me. They uttered a short reply, and our translator explained.

"They don't know what you're talking about."

I witness magic each time I visit Siberia. The vast steppe and tundra spaces are alive with energy and spiritual forces that dance through the immense skies and merge with the relentless winds.

Like the tundra, the open vistas of our lands are also not empty. They are filled with intelligent life energy. Yet just as tundra plants live in a fragile balance, as the ecosystems of our vast lands are threatened, it can feel like the strong spirits have left these places.

Tundra Reindeer inspire us to call the magic back.

Ceremonies, vision quests, and spiritual practices invoke magic as they bring us into harmony with natural living forces. Grace can also appear at any time, as the creative spirit of life is with and around us, no matter where we are.

Last winter I was working a lot with little time outside because of the shorter days. One night, when I was feeling sad about being inside so much, I had the feeling that I should look up. There on the window shelf sat my cactus plant, bursting with glowing red buds like a lit Christmas tree. The cactus hadn't bloomed in a year. Nature felt so close in those moments. The next morning, I had to search for the buds that appeared to be illuminated the night before. I checked later after dark to see if the indoor lights had made them glow. They looked like common blossoms. I had seen the spiritual light of this plant.

Another time, I was heartbroken as so many trees were being cut near where I live. My son, Eben, and I ventured onto the beach. The sky stretched over the water to mountains in the north, east, and west. Amidst the blue was a layering of clouds whose edges were etched in golden sunlight. Eben and I looked up in awe, then we suddenly stopped. The blue transformed before our eyes into a luminous turquoise. The water was burgundy. The clouds were dazzling in form and color. I got dizzy looking up; I felt like I was in a dream. The vast sky was illumined with color, as if we were looking through a colored filter. In all my years and travels, I have never seen a sky like this—was the spiritual light of the felled trees illuminating the heavens? The miracle lasted seven minutes.

When I was a teenager, my parents moved me and my four younger siblings to a small house on the outskirts of town. I was often overwhelmed living in humble spaces with a large family that suffered daily challenges. Yet, this house sat on a wooded lot, surrounded by trees. Nature was a calming presence. Each morning, I listened to a phoebe bird, whose song still stirs me. Within a year, the trees were cleared to make room for a garden and a play area for the younger children. The earth shuddered. The spirited harmony of the forest and the phoebe were gone.

Little soothes the pain we can feel when beloved trees are felled. It is not only trees we lose but animals, birds, insects, and other woodland beings. Yet, when I feel despairing or disconnected from nature, there often appear signs that lift my spirit. I feel these omens are the Earth saying: "You are always one with nature!" and "Don't give up—don't lose hope!"

The true nature of reality is miraculous beyond what we can fathom. The spirit of Tundra Reindeer connects us with this creative force, even during the times we find most painful.

Unlike any other members of the deer family, both male and female reindeer grow antlers. Just as with shamans of the far north, we can fly with the Reindeer spirit, even travel during our bleakest moments through the cosmic pathways of its antlers to feel refreshed by the boundless spirit of life.

Imagine yourself rooted in a strong Reindeer body. Feel the goodness and solidity of this body and four stable feet upon the earth. Take your time with this. When you feel oneness with a healthy Reindeer spirit, lift your vision—travel with your awareness up through Reindeer antlers to explore the spacious skies. Sense the immense blue atmosphere. Then open to the depth of space beyond the blue of the skies. Sense infinite layers of stars. Rest with your whole being in this rich, limitless space. Allow the mystery to absorb and replenish you.

I began journeying with Tundra Reindeer when I shadowed a Nenets daughter herding reindeer on the tundra one morning. After having a traumatic vertigo episode where I had collapsed in Heathrow Airport on my travels to Moscow, I still felt unstable and anxious. I stayed a distance behind the girl on the tundra. Mostly we sat watching the reindeer graze. At times we skipped across stones and small boggy areas, following the large herd as it moved. It was beautiful to watch the young herder who was so at home on the land and with the animals. As we were close to the reindeer, I smelled their odor and could see the tufts on their fur coats. I felt their spirit. Being on vast tundra lands with the reindeer and Nenets daughter that morning eased my own spirit.

Since this time, I journey with Tundra Reindeer to get grounded and to revive. The expansive perspectives I gain are always helpful.

In the spring, when they are beginning to grow, reindeer antlers are covered in a soft, spongy skin called velvet. Within the year, the antlers mineralize into bone. The males can grow a crown that in full maturity may span over four feet in both width and length. Reindeer antlers are the largest and heaviest of any animal that carries antlers. Only the strong and healthy reindeer can carry the great antler sets that may weigh up to forty pounds.

Each year, the reindeer releases it majestic and cosmic antlers back to nourish the earth and new antlers begin to grow. In the same way, we can stay humble, offering ourselves back to the earth and caring for nature. If we accept and celebrate our connection to the earth, the magic that is dormant within us will effortlessly grow.

The lichen reindeer dig for under the ice and snow with their hooves and antlers to nourish them through the endless winter season is an ancient form of life. Nutrient-rich lichen, whose branches look like tiny antlers, is the heart of the tundra. It feeds the largest animal of these lands, and it covers the rocks as it breaks them down to create fertile soil. This is the only way topsoil can be made on the tundra, as there's not enough plant life in these barren lands to do this work of making the soil.

We all know what it's like to have to break through stiff or cold parts of us to get to tender, hidden aspects of who we really are. Just as snow is an insulator, emotional barriers form to protect us—yet over time, they disconnect us from our heart, just as ice can prevent a tundra reindeer from being able to dig through to the lichen they eat to survive.

As we soften the hardened places within us, we will find what feeds our heart.

Tundra reindeer eyes are golden-brown in the summer and changing to violet as the days become shorter; then blue through the winter, which allows them to see in continuous darkness. This ally encourages us to look for the grace within personal and collective dark nights, to break through frozen parts of us to heal our heart—and to dig through encrusted societal values to live in harmony with our amazing planet.

Tundra reindeer find everything they need to thrive on a vast, frozen landscape. As we call upon its medicine to help us transform, it guides us back to our internal light and to the vastly rich terrain of the creative spirit of life.

Practice

Tundra Reindeer, with its majestic antlers that feel into rich cosmic spaces, teaches us to reconnect with the mystery that is all around us all the time—lighting the path through the dark as we wake up to our miraculous world.

The simplest way to invite the creative spirit into our lives is to honor the nature with which we share this earthly experience. Commit to engage the nature you live with as alive and aware: trees, plants, stones, water bodies, animals, birds, and insects. Acknowledge the land and sky spaces. Observe seasonal as well as daily rhythms. Appreciate and speak with all aspects of nature, including the wind, sun, moon, and starlight. All are conscious and receptive to your energy and attention.

Over time, you will witness the synchronicity and magic that occur each day, small and large. The more you engage this, the richer and more textured life will feel. Let these relationships grow as nature does, at their own pace.

To make room within us for the sacred to blossom, we can also soften how we relate with linear time. Choose a day to pay extra attention to clock time. You will notice how some minutes or hours seem to pass by quickly, while others seem to move very slowly. Remember a day when you felt pressured by schedules, deadlines, or appointments. What were you aware of that day? Did time seem to press in on you?

Now, remember a day when you felt out of time. You may have been walking in nature; doing yoga or meditating; playing with your child or grandchild or favorite animal friend; absorbed in a creative project or a daydream. Did time move slowly? Did you lose track of time altogether? What did you notice? Did you feel a sense of goodness, or was there a sparkle in the space around you?

These are some qualities we may experience as we open to natural time.

Here are other simple ways to invite the richness of space into daily life:

- Light a candle and sit for a while as the sun rises and sets.

- On a busy day, close your eyes in free moments and take a few nice, deep breaths. Open to the rich spaces inside of and all around you.

- If you're working at a computer, close your eyes at free moments and imagine your feet upon ancient pathways that reindeer and reindeer people have followed for centuries. Envision that you run through the vast tundra spaces, feeling the winds and life force all around you. Feel possibility come alive.

- Take breaks in your day and weeks to be outside at a park or in nature. Be relaxed, feeling your body glide through space as you walk, opening to the sounds, scents, beauty, and subtle qualities that surround you.

- Look up to the sky frequently to renew your sense of wonder. Invite communication with the vast and conscious universe that we are one with.

- If you're inside or in a city, enjoy the company of a favorite plant. Or gaze out to the trees or sky outside your window.

Think of other ways to open space in your mind and heart. Create open, restful times that invite richness into everyday life.

As you open to natural time, the moments will begin to feel expansive.

At other times, you may like to move your body to activate the light and energy within and all around you.

Plant your reindeer feet firmly on the floor or on the earth to first feel grounded. Then move your hands, fingers, arms, and body as if they are antlers flowing from the crown like rivulets. Relax your mind and move slowly; let your body guide you. Follow the flow of reindeer antlers, opening to sense the energy rising through you from the earth, telluric forces that merge with the cosmic flow down through your crown from the heavens. Feel yourself as a conduit to deep currents of life from the Earth and heavens that merge in your heart. Feel the light pour through and radiate from your heart as your body moves, feeling oneness with the vibrant energy in the spaces all around you.

You may like to draw or paint or mold Tundra Reindeer antler designs with clay. Or simply trace them with your fingers in the space in front of you, in the air. Even small movements can help us breathe more fully and unravel bound places inside.

We can also create a restful internal space by being still. Try sitting and taking a nice, deep breath. Then thank your mind for all it does. Tell it how grateful you are, and it will relax.

"Thank you, mind. I am so grateful for everything you do."

Now, take twelve more gentle, focused breaths as you sense the grace within you and in the space around you. It's always there, even when it doesn't seem so or when you forget. Hold space for your own light and the possibility of miracles.

As our internal light grows, we naturally radiate compassionate energy. We can hold the gentle intention for this energy to benefit people who are separated from their nomadic identity and ancestral lands, tundra reindeer affected by climate change, and fragile ecosystems impacted by pollution and exploitation. To make these offerings tangible, consider supporting organizations that preserve the wisdom and ancestral lands of ancient indigenous peoples.

CHAPTER 3
Sun and Moon

Sandra

> I am walking through desolate lands, with no light other than
> the sun, moon, and stars to help me find my way.

What I described of desolate lands is a metaphor that can feel quite
real to us in our own life when we feel no support while walking
through the darkness of life. In these times, it is important to remember the sun is always shining down upon us, creating a path that can
guide us through some of the brambles of life that we so often can get
caught in.

The moon bestows upon us her loving embrace, teaching us about
the power of her cycles, of going dark and of growing back into her
fullness. Learning from the moon helps us to navigate our way through

life's challenges and, teaches us about right timing and how we can join with the moon for exponential spiritual power. If we focus on the power of the moon during our spiritual work, the moon will always enlighten us and guide us on our next steps.

Even if you feel like you have been walking in darkness, remember that you will exit. Just as nature has her phases and cycles, which always spiral into another cycle, you will exit. The moon, through her changing phases and light, teaches us how to pace ourselves and how to get back into the flow of life. When our ego is pulling us in so many directions, we enter chaos. The moon will bring you back to your center once you learn how to follow her changing phases, which match your own changing phases. The same is true with the sun, as we can mark time by its cycles, which are the same as our own internal cycles. Working with cycles of the sun and moon will put us in harmony with the river of life.

In certain processes, the sun and moon need to be joined, as the male and female, to create a new seed to plant, in order to grow, as we perform ceremonial work. Both the sun and moon are always there for us as natural allies.

In the world of the shaman, the night sky is the ally that is used for knowing the best timing for preparing for ceremonial work. By watching the phases of the moon, the cycles of the sun, and the constellations, the shamans tap into the most profound time for creating a ceremony, a ceremony that will use intention, spirit, and heart, to invoke healing or to ask for some change in life to occur. Ceremony is used to honor all changes, transitions, celebrations, and tragedies and to restore balance. When we perform ceremonies, we invoke our inner spirit to align with the creative forces of the universe to make our dreams so.

In the world of the shaman, ceremony is a sacred act. Ceremony puts us back into a strong connection with the divine and is where an energy field is created so that good things come our way and healing occurs. Ceremonies to mark a change in this way have been performed all over the world and still are today.

Once we return our love, energy, and commitment to the divine forces surrounding all of us, we enter the flow of life. Once we enter the flow of life—versus trying to control all the outcomes in our life— we then are in a state of surrender, where we can be open to spiritual forces that provide guidance and healing and restore balance.

Shamans are gardeners of energy who, using spirit-led ceremonies, cultivate, tend, and nourish formless energies that will be created into physical form in the tangible realms. Those of you who are gardeners know the importance of planting in accordance with both the cycles of the sun and the phases of the moon to manifest the healthiest growth.

The sun, which is billions of years old, fills our bodies with the energy it needs to thrive in life and grow into healthy beings. Sunlight is in plants and trees, so when we eat them, we receive more sunlight, which is utilized for our nurturance and health.

In just about every shamanic culture I know of, the sun has been greeted upon awakening. You can only imagine how, without electricity, people looked forward to the sun gracing them each day. The Egyptians worshipped the sacred scarab, who spends its life rolling dung, symbolizing rebirth and creation. As the sun rises and sets each day, it provides an opportunity for us to be reborn.

There are so many stories about the moon and how it rules our emotions and the tides. We love to sing to the moon, to watch the magic of the new crescent forming, and we are in awe of the full moon in all its beauty. We love the stories of how every full moon shines different qualities on the Earth, like the harvest moon whose light is an intense bright orange and reminds us it is time to harvest all we planted in our inner and outer landscape. We all are in awe of the big red-orange moon shining down on us. As the harvest moon is known to rule our planting phases, it can remind us of a simpler way of life. And I find many people find a particular magic when the harvest moon shines her bright light, reminding us that a new time of change is coming and that we are truly connected to Nature.

A little background of what happened in my life:

Due to taking on the pain of so many people, I eventually found myself existing in a world in which I did not want to live. I was such an empath, and I wanted to relieve people of their pain. Of course, this was one of life's little illusions about which I had not yet learned. There is no way to take away the pain of another. What we can do is hold space for them, such as by performing little ceremonies for them like lighting a candle for them each day, thinking kind thoughts about them, or imagining a day when they will be happy. But we can't take away their pain.

Once I reached puberty, I had a lot of suicidal thoughts that lasted a good part of my adult years, until the 1980s, when I had the incredible opportunity to learn shamanic journeying. One of the most common ceremonies and practices in shamanism is the shamanic journey, where we have access to divine helping spirits who can provide guidance and healing.

In one of my very first journeys, I went to my divine helping spirit for a visit. It is a common practice in shamanism to visit one's helping spirits without asking for any help or for favors. In this journey, my helping spirit and I were chatting like old friends. He said to me, "Whatever you do in life, never sit down in the dark." That was the end of the journey.

I was living in San Francisco and had developed a strong mentoring relationship with my teacher, who at the time was a great shaman. I went out to dinner with him and shared with him my journey. And then he closed his eyes. His eyes were glassy when he reopened them. This is common when someone journeys and is in an altered state of consciousness. So, he had let his typical mental state go for a minute and dropped into his intuition. I could see he was looking very far away.

He looked across the table and said, "You are going to be a great shaman one day."

I did devote my life to the practice of shamanism and have taught tens of thousands of people about this ancient practice and how to bridge it into our lives today. But still, one of the most poignant journeys in my more than forty years of practicing shamanism was the one in which my guardian spirit advised me not to sit down in the dark. I was to learn over time that just as the sun and moon rise and set, cycles in life move in a similar fashion. We have "moon" phases in life when we need time for reflection and inner work. It is the moon who guides us to go deep within. We have "sun" cycles in which new things are born and we must take chances and create new relationships. The cycles of the sun remind us that, in nature, everything changes. Nothing in nature is stagnant. This can be really unsettling. And we need the warmth of the sun to remind us of that. Although the shadow is part of life, the sun does return every day, lighting up cells, revitalizing our life force and soul, and keeping us alive.

This is important to remember during initiations. I know it has been important to me because many times in life I became so paralyzed by what was happening in my life, in the world, or both. And I did want to sit down or go to bed and pull the covers over my head until "it" was all over. But, since the beginning of time, we all are under the ever-changing phases of the moon and the sun, and of course I don't want to leave out the stars.

Initiation times can be very lonely because it is time for you to chip away at your ego and discover your true spiritual identity and strength. No one can help you find your spiritual strength. This is a job only you can do.

If you practice shamanic journeying, you may have noticed that in certain times of transformation, the helping spirits become uncommunicative with you. You can feel their presence, but you can't hear their guidance. It feels like you have been deserted. In truth, the helping spirits know the powers you have, the powers you might have forgotten, when you are feeling small and insignificant in your human body.

Family, friends, and the divine can stand by to cheer you on. But your allies are the ones who become your teachers, show you where to take your next step, and provide light in the dark.

One of the best tools to help you find a way to stand up and take a tiny step is ceremony. Raising your arms up to the sun and moon plants seeds that show the way on the next step of your journey.

There will be plenty of sacred spots you can find in the Dark Night of the Soul to perform your ceremonies. There are fire pits, rocks, trees, plants, the wind, rivers, and the list goes on. These places become such important rest spots where you can perform your spiritual work so that you can cry, ask for help, or ask for an omen that will guide you to your next steps.

Ceremony also lets the spirits know where you became stuck so that they can provide whatever invisible help they have, to share at least a clue. Remember, there are no demons in the Dark Night of the Soul. There is nothing to fear in this mysterious territory and phase of life. You get to meet yourself fully during any type of initiation. You might have things you feel you need to work out. Ceremony is a good way to do this. Maybe you never had a ceremony to honor a transition in your life, such as becoming a teenager or a parent. Maybe a ceremony will aid you in letting go of your anger and fears. Maybe there is something from a past life that is burdening you, and a ceremony can free your psychic space so that you can fill it with more light. You can only imagine the things we carry around that burden us and keep us from moving forward in life. We feel so heavy from dragging our past around. It is almost like a chain holding us back.

The following are a few examples of a ceremony:

- **In the sand, draw a mandala representing something you wish to release and allow the ancient sea to wash your pain away.**

- **Use fire to burn up your old karma, betrayals, and hurts.**

- **Access the power of the wind to release you from what keeps you from taking flight in life.**

- **Ground yourself by touching the earth, which provides us with so much nurturance but is also happy to receive our burdens, just like she receives the falling leaves of autumn that return to her and act as compost.**

This energy is unusable, and it covers up the spirit that our intuition is trying to reveal to us.

Ceremony is the shaman's vehicle for creating change. And all shamans rely on the skies to guide them as to what is the best time of year to perform their ceremony and whether to work for an hour, all night, five days, and so on. Shamans are guided by the sun and the moon as to what elements should be brought in to help with the intention of the work.

Practice

As I shared, the challenges that we go through when navigating darkness are for our benefit because the experience changes us into more mature people with a better connection to our own inner world and the divine around us.

But as humans with egos that are easily bruised and traumatized, we often end up dragging around all the bad memories of what happened to us. If you look at the big picture, you have experienced traumas in your past lives as well as in the present. You and your ancestors might have been part of atrocities that occurred in the past and that you need to resolve to be free. You might have been betrayed in this lifetime or in a past life. Do you have issues with self-worth? Because if we do not love ourselves, it is a betrayal to our soul and to Creator.

To be free to move ahead, without old memories acting like shackles that anchor you to old injuries, is such a relief. And when you acknowledge that you are past these old memories, it is time to acknowledge what happened and to release the pain to find freedom.

You are going to have the opportunity to explore different timelines.

You can do this practice multiple times, in pieces, so that you are not overwhelmed by doing it all in one journey. Or you can release everything immediately and feel the relief of dropping your burdens.

You will look at who your acts and deeds harmed and what hurts or betrayals in both the past and the present are still impacting you. Then you will look into the future, from where you are in the present, and you might be able to see something, an act you might do in the future, for a particular reason, that might end up harming people. You are cleaning all this old, present, and future energy to create a clear space to walk through in life. Some of us feel burdened by our past and present. Some of us souls have been here for so many thousands of years. Think of all the experiences, all the atrocities, all the wars, all the violence, but all the great things, the good deeds we did to help people. We have a long history.

Most of all we must let go of how hard we are on ourselves and learn the power of unconditional love for the self.

Use a favorite track of spiritual music without words to help you move into a spiritual state and to leave your ego and everyday life behind.

You're going to have the opportunity to gaze upon your past lives, your present, and possible future lives. Engage your heart center, your third eye, and your hands. Think of your favorite color of light. Send and radiate this light out of your hands and out of your heart, directing it to the sources of troubling events. You're going to send that light as bubbles. The wind is going to be your ally, taking those bubbles and then bursting them. All those memories of the past are gone. They don't exist anymore.

You will imagine letting go of your body, as if you were taking off a coat, and experiencing the divine light flowing inside you. This is the same light that the Divine created you with. This is your spirit, and your spirit is all-knowing, just like Creator.

Go deep into this spiritual light. You were born with the same spiritual light that Creator shines upon all of life, that light that the sun shines upon all of life every day. You are sunlight. You are starlight. You are moonlight. Let that light flow through your body.

In the practice of shamanism, intention and imagination are your spirit's way to travel. Hold the intention, and use your imagination to see, feel, and experience yourself in some way being transported to the Land of Forgiveness.

Once you arrive at the Land of Forgiveness, find a good flat place to stand on the road so that you feel steady and solid. You will find yourself on a long, straight road. Behind you, you can see a similarly long, windy road that goes on forever. And a long road continues in front of you. It also looks like it goes on forever. Call upon the wind to come and meet you as an ally who will be doing some very powerful work with you. The wind comes and kisses your cheek. It's ready to help.

For the next step, you'll experience your inner light. This is the inner light that is beyond your ego. This light is like starlight, sunlight, moonlight. You're going to let this beautiful light flow throughout your entire body.

Start to look back at your past. With your third eye opened, gently skim your past. Don't let yourself be bogged down by the story. Don't get stuck in your past. Open your heart. Open the light flowing out of your hands. With your third eye, start to get a sense of the energies from the past that need to be cleansed, discreated, uncreated, dissolved, dismembered, destroyed. In that lifetime or in that event of the past, you received a great learning. It might have been a painful learning, but it helped you move into your true growth. With your heart, with your hands, and with your third eye, send out bubbles of light of your favorite healing color, completely covering the past.

But we also don't want to get lost in the energy of denial. Your third eye might pick up an actual, true tragic event, one that you need to go back and process, to ask for forgiveness, to ask for healing, or to forgive yourself. Remember, one of the most important tools of the journey that we're on is the ability to forgive ourselves.

Bring intention and focus on the past, allowing those bubbles to break up memories that no longer need to be held in your cellular makeup. Find the most healing color, and working with the wind, just let those memories go. Let the wind blow those bubbles up to the creative forces of the universe, who transmute all this energy into love and more light. Look back on the path you just cleared. Gaze upon the lovely, beautiful plants, herbs, and flowers now growing throughout that path, thanks to your willingness to remove so much of that human history we don't need to keep hanging on to anymore. We are at a different time on the planet. We have different issues. Absorb the beauty. Feel how your heart feels from clearing all the old pains, hurts, and abuses. If you need to, go back and finish the work at another time.

For now, it's time to move to our present. We put our arms up. We face the sun. We now look at our present. A screen appears. We can see a life review in which we can witness past events where we were harmed, hurt another, lied, or worked without integrity. While breathing deeply and with an open heart, allow the wind to carry each memory up to the creative forces of the universe to be uncreated, discreated, dismembered, dissolved, destroyed. Again, you can come back to a particular event that you need to work on later.

Now it is time to turn to the future. This can get confusing to our rational mind, as the future has not occurred yet. But let's create a beautiful future for ourselves. We want to heal and forgive any potential hurts that we might be part of in the future.

Breathe out of your heart, and allow those healing bubbles of your favorite color to break up and clear out any future harm that might become an obstacle on your path. Clear the energy. We do this for ourselves and for the collective. Our collective reflects the hurts we are holding. Our inner world is always reflected in the outer world.

We eat so much anger, hate, fear, and self-loathing. Now it is time to eat and digest the beauty of life. It's time to start loving ourselves.

It is time to show kindness, forgiveness, and compassion for others. We still need to process our deep hurts. But at some point, we need to let them go so that they can be replaced by the beauty of life and new opportunities for our future.

Repeat this work as often as you need to in order to feel like the energies are clear all around you. You have created a beautiful new field of energy to step into for yourself and to live your soul's journey.

Releasing these old hurts and traumas opens a space inside of you—a sacred space for more good seeds to be planted in your inner garden and new dreams to materialize in your life. After releasing your old beliefs, thought forms, and patterns of disempowerment, imagine yourself filling up with the goodness of life: positive feelings, hope, light, love, kindness shown to you by others, and kindness to yourself.

You have let go of what no longer fills you with meaning and good health on any level.

As you complete this practice and repeat it, a new weaving with new vibrant and energetic threads in the unseen realms are woven together to create a new life plan for you.

CHAPTER 4
Bat

Llyn

While living in India at age twenty-six, I stayed for several months in a Franciscan ashram. The enclave was surrounded by trees, and its internal gardens gave the air a delicately sweet scent. The haven attracted people from all over the world who came to study yoga and Eastern mysticism. The seekers gathered every evening to share what they were learning and experiencing. The Franciscans spent their own free time in silent reflection and in nature.

At dusk, nuns dressed in simple brown habits climbed the wooden ladder that leaned against the far end of the ashram building. Each found their spot on the flat-topped roof, where, sitting cross-legged, they meditated. The nuns of my Catholic school years had a rigid decorum, which made the folksiness of the Franciscans so refreshing.

The sisters sat as dark silhouettes against the sunset-painted skies. Just as mystics of ages gone by, they merged with the magical time of day before night descended. Hundreds of black forms releasing from the tree boughs flitted by them—the dimming skies teemed with bats.

No matter where in the wild we are, as daylight morphs into darkness, nature seems to come alive. As the sun sets, we may feel the wind stir and see bats dart through the darkening space. We may hear the purest melodies of evening birds just as their nocturnal friends are waking up for the night's hunt. If the skies are clear, the stars will become visible.

Just as dusk is a magical, transitional time of shifting and changing, the spirit of Bat guides us to transform through the transitional times in our lives.

Many people associate bats with fear, as they remind us of what lies in the unknown, hidden places of the dark night. They carry diseases that are deadly to humans. And though it is rare, common vampire bats of tropical and subtropical regions of northern Mexico and parts of South America prey on livestock—and, as humans destroy their forest habitats, the vampire bats sometimes prey on people who are sleeping out in the open air.

Bat can trigger in us a sense of danger, terror, and even threat of death. It is a fierce medicine forcing us to face our fears and transform what holds us back. This is related to shamanic initiation.

Bats live in trees and in caves. Shamans have conducted initiatory rites and ceremonies in caves since time immemorial.

In 1999, my colleague, Bill Pfeiffer, and I stood with a *shamanka* (a female Siberian shaman) and her two apprentices at an ancient cave site. The entrance didn't appear wide enough to fit the largest of us. We were to climb in through the stone hole, then creep on hands and knees through a narrow, roughly hewn tunnel. Everyone was ready, each of us with a large battery pack strapped to the waist and a headlamp on. I asked for a moment to be alone and wandered off to where I couldn't be seen. My heart pounded. My body shook. I thought I would throw up. I took very slow, deep breaths until I felt the spirit of the cave.

Once inside, we inched through the tight stone corridor. After what felt like forever, holding a rope, we slid one by one down a ledge that led us to the inner chamber of the cave. We each found our place, then lights out, we sat in silent darkness. In the dreamscape of the earth's womb, I met ancestors who since the Stone Age had performed sacred rituals in this cave.

Retracing our pilgrimage was risky. Yet as we crawled back through the canal, I felt as solid as the stone that encased us. Emerging into daylight, we were reborn.

Most of us haven't grown up in communities that married us to the land and spirits through ceremony. We haven't been guided through initiations that shamanic peoples have performed all over this planet since the beginning of humanity. In modern life, our illnesses, accidents, depressions, and losses are the initiations. Yet, this is resonant with ancient ways.

On one Siberia trip, Bill Pfeiffer and I met with the few *kam* (shamans) remaining in Mountainous Shoria. We had tea in the humble home of one man in his eighties. Laying next to him on a small rustic table was a bowlful of garlic. As we spoke together, the man popped into his mouth one garlic clove after another as if they were sweets. We asked him how shamans are recognized in the Shor tradition. The elder said the kam would only consider training someone who had the "shamanic illness" for three or more years, as this was how the spirits marked the shaman to be. The illness could be caused by an accident, or it could be a chronic or life-threatening sickness or a psychological crisis. The elder said the spirits were close to such people, and this direct link with spirit was needed to shamanize.

When things go wrong, the familiar drops away. Who we are, what life should be, what we need to do in the world—all are under question. Our basic sense of identity breaks down, like the shamanic illness, which is a death to the old self.

Bat invites us to open our subtle senses during dark times. We can call upon its spirit when, at critical life transitions, there are no elders around to read the signs and omens or tell us that the spirits are close or that our nervous breakdown, struggle through cancer, or other aspect of life that's fallen apart is a shamanic opening.

With its excellent hearing, echo sounding, and night vision, Bat helps us use our inner sight to wake up in a dark night to see that we are in an initiatory chamber.

When troubled or suffering, staying awake to the spirits that are near and believing there is meaning through whatever we experience can make all the difference. Whether or not we embrace shamanism, our hardships can activate our spiritual gifts. Some transformations happen quickly, yet, just as initiation is a beginning, most changes happen over time.

There are daily opportunities to evolve. Every outbreath is a death; every inbreath is like being reborn. Every gap between what was and what is not yet formed is a liminal space of possibility.

To get closer to our own potential, we can rest more within the gaps to touch what we really feel and transform what limits us. The spiritual power of Bat is about moving through fear and exposing what is hidden or suppressed.

At our first night around the campfire on wilderness retreats, I invite people to share what challenges them.

"I'm having a hard time moving beyond the loss of my father."

"I feel angry and hopeless about the species we've lost and the trees and forests being destroyed."

People at first appear shy, yet once sharing is underway, a felt sense of connection and caring comes into the circle.

If we could hear people's thoughts, we might imagine them saying: "It's okay to be struggling—no one is judging me." "I can say what I really feel and be heard."

Being vulnerable gets us out of our heads and into our hearts, and it's grounding to see that we share similar situations and concerns. We're all on a very human journey.

If we're not in touch with what we feel, we can practice. When you detect a nuance of feeling, scan your body: What sensations do you notice, and where? Place your palms on this part of your body, and take a few soft, steady breaths. Then, say out loud what's in your heart.

Feelings are not right or wrong; they are just what we feel. It's what we do with them that matters. We might feel embarrassed by what we say, or think we should only state what is positive. Yet, in this private truth-telling moment, notice if your heart settles and breathing is deeper just in being real. The mind has all kinds of convolutions, yet our body tells the truth through how we move, gesture, and breathe. It relaxes when we're authentic.

When we allow and speak what we usually keep down, we get to know ourselves better. We can make friends with what we feel, so we don't see our obstacles or weaknesses as someone else's, not understanding they are ours. We can practice communicating feelings that are hard to express.

In voicing my feelings, they can shift. I might begin by feeling agitated or fearful yet break down in tears as I touch underlying sadness. Some feelings aren't as threatening as I thought. Others evaporate as I voice them. Subtle moods may hold intuitive messages or disguise what's most difficult, such as aspects of myself I dislike or that might even terrify me.

Coming face to face with my fears and blind spots can make me feel like I'm standing outside on a raw, windy night with nothing but my boots on. The chill running up my spine tells me something is about to die. I'm afraid it's me. Yet, just as the destiny of a wave is a cold and crashing death, the wave doesn't rest at the shore. After crashing, the water ebbs like an inbreath before the next upswelling. Stand at the water's edge, and you will feel this creative changeover as waves crash, retreat, and then rise again.

Bat medicine tells us the old ways are over. It reassures us that as form is very changeable at threshold places, we can change at our own edges.

As waves of life crash, our dreads and demons can come out. This is a good time to be curious about what we avoid in ourselves. Yet, we need to feel calm enough to look inside. Like the gap as the sea retreats, we can take a deep breath at the thresholds, take the time to be gentle and get to know ourselves better. In being tender and listening to the parts of us that are angry and afraid, these lost ones can settle into the whole of us.

Just as personal shadows feel intense, we can feel overwhelmed by hidden aspects of humanity that are more visible in erratic times. All that is painful in our world now pushes us to embrace greater wholeness.

The shamanic path is marked by spiritual capacities that arise through dismemberment, the shamanic death. Bat medicine shows that the fragmentation of our world is also a dissolution that unleashes power.

This is not time to give up, but rather to honor what is in our hearts and call in the life we truly long for.

In this mutable period of reality shifting, what we dream and give our good energy to nourishes a more wholesome reality. Just as shamans are called by spirit to use their powers to keep harmony between people, spirit, and nature, we can rise from the ashes of our shamanic deaths to fulfill our calling and do what's in our power to nurture life.

Although it conveys fierce medicine, the mother bat is nurturing with her young. She gestates one unborn child at a time, occasionally twins. The mother hangs upside down while she is giving birth, so the baby is born against the pull of gravity. As the tiny bat body emerges, it drops—the mother must instinctively catch the newborn in her wings, or it falls to its death. The feminine aspect of Bat encourages us to accept the time we need to grow and promises to catch us in her wings as we're ready to let go and birth new ways, precarious as that change may feel.

The gestation period for a developing bat is three to seven months, depending on the species. Babies grow and birth in darkness.

Dark nights can develop and breathe new possibilities to life, yet how long do we incubate, how much must we endure as these new changes are born?

We may never fully grasp another's anguish. Our attention and care make a difference, though there are times when nothing seems to help. Those who make it through initiations often return renewed with clearer purpose. Yet, it's heartbreaking and tragic when a loved one doesn't return from the initiation cave and seems to be lost. Bat teaches us to respect every journey and reminds us in those circumstances that more is happening than we understand. When the situation appears dire, Bat opens our inner sight so we can sense that the light is still there. From a spiritual perspective, our loved one may have taken on a deep task in this lifetime. We can light candles, pray, make offerings on the person's behalf, and call out their name in the spiritual realms, encouraging them to come home to themselves. We can envision this person surrounded by compassionate forces and divine light. Ultimately, each person alone must find their way.

Shamanic illness is a death leading to a new spiritual form. This is also true with physical death.

When Bat came into my life, I sensed that someone close to me would die. I struggled with this foreboding thought until, through working with the spirit of Bat, I felt at peace. Some weeks later, a good friend unexpectedly died, a man I'd known and worked with for twenty-five years. He was such a kind and humorous person. Memories of our many happy times together overwhelmed me. I could see my friend's impish smile and his blue eyes so clearly through my tears.

Loss and grief are real. Yet, knowing the death of someone dear to me hovered in the ethers well before it happened—as I gained spiritual perspective from Bat—my heart did settle.

The call to transform, pass from one form into another, is part of life. Whether through death, illness, or change, it may reverberate for days or years. Just as signs indicate shamanic death, the web of life vibrates when one is to pass through the veils into a new experience. Bat, who hangs upside down even upon death, is a prime ally to help us see the imprints that foretell form-changing—and to fear it less. Fear shrouds the light and beauty of the most significant shapeshift we know: death.

Just as dusk is a magical time of changing forms, Bat helps us transform through life's transitions. It shows us that as we embrace what we hide—the shadow aspects of self—as we shift ourselves and our world to greater wholeness.

Through deepening our relationship with ourselves and the Earth, we energize our good wishes for nature. To make these wishes real, we can honor Bat by building bat houses for these animals, educating children and neighbors about the amazing qualities of bats and their importance as part of healthy ecosystems. We can plant trees and help preserve forests, as trees are where many bat species live.

Practice

This active imagining practice helps us stay centered and embodied as we transform through our challenges.

Sit or lie comfortably in a protected space. Take a few deep breaths.

Then, breathing normally, relax a little more with each breath out.

Now, feel, sense, or see yourself standing at the mouth of an initiation cave.

What do you want to take into the cave with you? Examples are cornmeal or tobacco offerings, a candle, or other items that feel sacred to you. You may also want to have practical tools on hand such as a headlamp, food, water, or a mat to sit on.

Would you like to take a wool blanket or sweater for warmth? Are you wearing the right footwear?

Watch as what you need to support your journey spontaneously appears as you stand at the cave's mouth, as it can also do once you are inside.

Now, feel Bat nearby.

Also call in any other spiritual presences that feel right. What good spirits are close to you?

Do you want to imagine a friend or loved one by your side?

Take a few moments to feel who will accompany you into the darkness.

Also, who will hold space for you and guard the cave's entrance? This person or spirit will pray for you. They will also be the one to welcome you when you step back through the portal, out of darkness and into light.

Feel the love and care of these allies you have chosen and those who naturally show up at any time to support you. Feel the living field of light and goodness that surrounds you. Make it real.

With powerful allies supporting you, think on your higher intentions during this time in life. What would you wish for? In reflecting, carefully view from every angle what you desire. See in your mind's eye pictures, scenes, and images related to your intentions.

You may want to heal emotionally or be physically well again. You may want to regain financial stability. You may want to have courage and become stronger. You may want to set upon a daunting new life course.

Let the thoughts, pictures, and images connected with your intentions absorb you; make them vivid. Take all the time you like seeing these in your mind's eye.

Now, imagine the thoughts and images becoming pure energy. Feel this energy wash through your mind. You may see color or sense a diffuse white light.

The cloud of energy completely fills your head and mind. Notice the sensations.

When you are ready, feel the energy of your intentions drop from your head, through your throat, and into your heart. This energy floods your heart. Feel the energy of your intentions in your heart center.

Take your time.

When the feelings are strong, allow this cloud of light—intentions—to spread out from your heart and permeate every part of you to infuse your body.

Take all the time you like. Feel the goodness.

Feel your while being as one with your intentions.

If you are weak or feel afraid or confused, imagine that the strength, power, and energy of your intentions absorb these difficult feelings. Take your time until you feel oneness with your intent, from the top of your head to the tips of your fingers and toes, regardless of your circumstances.

Every part of you is saturated with the energy of your intentions.

You are your intent.

Feel the power, strength, and energy available: that is you.

When you are ready, one with your intent, fortified with everything you need, and feeling the spirits close, sprinkle offerings at the threshold.

Step through the entrance. Step into the mystery.

In the soft, dark interior of the cave, take time to study the stone walls. Notice everything. Feel the ancient ones. Feel the power of this place.

Now, remember what is happening in your life just as it is. Feel it all with you in this ancient space. Recognize that you are being initiated.

You have crossed a threshold. You stand in a crack between worlds, an opening to new expression. Everything happening in your life now has brought you to walk the sacred shaman's death, which will lead to some form of rebirth.

You have everything you need: mundane and sacred tools and your good spirit helpers. Whatever else you need on this journey will appear.

Feel the power, strength, and energy of your intentions throughout your whole being.

Take time to look at your challenges as if you were a bat hanging upside down, seeing your life from a different perspective. Ask Bat and the spirits to show you limiting stories that hold you back. See the stories that wrap around and limit you fall away so that more of your light can shine.

What do you sense? What do you feel?

Take all the time you like.

You can bring this experience to a close when it feels right. You may stay in the initiation cave of your life experience with tools and allies close. If you step back into daylight, make offerings as you leave. The gatekeeper will greet you.

Gently stretch. Become aware of your body in the room. Drink a glass of water. You may want to write or draw in a journal. Reflect on how you may bring the teachings of what you experienced in the journey space into your everyday life circumstances. Today or the next day, take a leisurely walk. Offer cornmeal or tobacco to your favorite tree or to the earth and express your gratitude.

We can bring the power of initiation to any difficult aspect of ordinary life. As we refine our intentions and merge each day with their strength and power, we invite ordinary magic, grace, to come alive.

CHAPTER 5

Octopus

Sandra

During your pilgrimage into the Dark Night of the Soul, you might find that the chaos and noise of the ordinary world are pulling much needed strength and energy from you.

Beings in nature, when they need to heal, tend to go into hibernation or into the dark to find quiet and stillness. Once we enter the darkness, a different part of us turns on. Our spirit starts to awaken and energizes us with our own light—the reflection of the light of Creator. And our non-ordinary senses start to slowly turn on. Your non-ordinary senses are the heightened senses of seeing with your invisible eyes, hearing with your non-ordinary ears, tapping into your gift of clairsentience. Our senses are heightened in the unseen and non-ordinary worlds. Even our senses of smell and taste become heightened when we step into the invisible worlds also known as the non-ordinary, unseen realms—the Other Worlds and the Dreamtime. Different cultures have different names for the home of the helping spirits they work with.

We tend to allow ourselves to be fed information from the outside world. As we have learned, with trickster energy, this can lead us off our path and sometimes have us moving in directions that are not healthy for us.

During my time of teaching shamanism, I have seen two different types of individuals. There are those who care to be around other people. They don't want to leave a group, not even during break time, because they are afraid of missing something. And then there are the people who are "lone wolves."

When we dive deep into the silence and darkness of the sea, we find an entire world full of the most amazing colorful beings, the likes of which we rarely see on earth, gliding gracefully alone in the depths of our great Mother Sea. Here they are in complete darkness and silence, yet they have ways of navigating with the other senses with which they were endowed as part of their physical makeup. They are so beautiful to gaze at, and they create so much wonder in us. It is as if the sea has treasures so different from what we have imagined while at the same time so beautiful, that we realize life is much bigger than we could have ever known.

Of course, for some, tapping into the immensity of our web of life can be quite overwhelming, so some people choose to befriend beings closer to home—those they are used to seeing.

I have always been a big fan of Octopus. Now, in recent times, Octopus has been gaining recognition in the world for its nature and intelligence. The film *My Octopus Teacher*, a documentary about this beautiful and fascinating animal, even won the Oscar in 2021.

A few years before the showing of this movie, I was gifted with a video to watch. A man on the beach had encountered an octopus that was stuck in the sand. He gently and slowly picked the octopus up and returned it to the sea. A few minutes later, the octopus swam to shore and slowly, with incredible effort, moved up on the sand. In the video, you can see how the octopus is struggling to do this. But in the end, it makes its way to the man who saved him. And in a truly sacred moment that made me cry, the octopus put one of its arms on this man's thick work boot as if to say, "Thank you for saving my life." It was so touching.

This reminded me of a new term being employed these days: "species loneliness." As humans, we watch the beings of nature through glass windows, cages, and cameras. We don't live such precious moments, such as the one in the video I watched, in which the octopus made such a huge effort to connect with its rescuer.

Octopuses are sea creatures that have captured the hearts of so many due to photos and videos of their mysterious ways and lives. They are seen as mysterious creatures of the sea. Although their ancestors seem to be squid, I have read articles where scientists wonder if they are from another planet.

Most octopuses have eight arms. But there are also tiny octopuses less than an inch that have webbing instead of arms. Their arms operate independently, enabling them to perform multiple tasks.

The species exists in so many different sizes—from less than an inch to sixteen feet! And I have seen photos of octopuses in a variety of unearthly colors. To hide, they can change colors. Octopuses can be fast swimmers, but they like to glide slowly and gracefully along the ocean floor. I can see myself living like this! To glide on the ocean floor and take in so much beauty and thus live my days, that would be a future I could imagine with joy!

Octopuses have an excellent sense of touch, and their suckers have receptacles to taste what they touch. This is an example of how other creatures make use of their senses.

We have the capability to use more of our senses in order to receive a deeper sense of the vibrancy of life all around us. We often feel dead inside or apathetic, and then everything around us seems to lack life and vitality. But in truth, we have senses that can absorb colors and frequencies we have never even imagined. We have become brainwashed by society teaching us how to live and follow the rules so as not to cause trouble. The act of doing this—acting as society wishes, against our natural instincts—cuts off the flow of energy, which also affects our ability to use our senses to pick up unseen colors and spirits of plants, animals, and so on. We can sense frequencies and the energy around us. But we are so distracted by the noise around us that we rarely use these senses.

I imagine myself living like an octopus who makes its home in a cave that it finds on the ocean floor.

There are many theories about the intelligence of octopuses. They seem to be very smart. I read one article that compared the intelligence of an octopus to a cat!

As humans, we believe we are the most intelligent species. But to watch how we destroy our own home planet and pollute that which gives us life—the Earth from which we get our food, the water we drink, and the air we breathe—it really makes me wonder! Since I feel that the intelligence of an octopus or cat is so much more evolved than that of humans, after reading the article comparing their intelligence, I found myself feeling insulted on their behalf.

In some ways, I am a very complex being. Like many sea creatures such as the octopus, I like being alone, gliding along the floor of the Earth, taking in all its beauty. Although I can run fast, I tend to walk and do my activities slowly. But like the octopus, I have a very social side. You can watch an octopus change colors when it encounters those toward which it has a pleasant feelings. But it can also turn bright red when it gets angry.

Living in a world so crowded and filled with noise from other people's psychic thoughts can be overwhelming. In addition, the noise and frequency of machines that surround us 24/7 results in a space where it is not always easy to find our own rhythm. I can feel like I am losing my mind in all the noise. When I must have silence, when I feel like I cannot live another day without it, I tend to escape to the sea and the ice.

Since I live in the desert, I can also find silence in the land. But there is something about being beside the cold ice, with ocean creatures, that brings peace to my soul. It is really through the profound silence, such as in the deep sea, that our psychic senses awaken, giving us a new perception on life.

I know that, just like every creature who lives on this Earth, octopuses have challenges. But the grace by which Octopus navigates through its life in the profound silence is so beautiful to watch. When we observe those amazing sea creatures that live deep in the sea, a feeling of peace washes over us. Their sheer grace is incredible.

I wonder what kind of graceful moments we can start creating in our own lives if we allow ourselves to step into the collective field of silence. What kind of healing can happen? And what gifts can we return with?

In the early 1990s, I had a mysterious illness that no one could diagnose. I went to doctors and of course also saw a wealth of shamanic practitioners, none of whom were able to help me. Because no one was getting how I was feeling, I felt sad and I felt such a lack of support.

I finally turned to the mushroom people, as I call psilocybin mushrooms. For some reason, they remind me of Octopus. Something about their frequency, how they vibrate, I don't know what it is, but I love them and see them as these sweet beings that are here to help in unseen ways. We know the magic of what mushrooms can do.

The reason I am sharing this is, as I mentioned, that Octopus is in touch with its senses; but because we are not, we miss spiritual messages and omens. We miss the beauty of colors that only "evolved" eyes can see. And as we are not sensitive enough to perceive them, we miss in our everyday lives seeing the invisible beings that play on Earth. Children can. Creatures like Octopus can. But we don't.

During the time that I was being healed by the mushrooms—and they did completely heal me—I was shown something extraordinary. In my bedroom, where I was lying quietly during my sacred healing ceremony, I have large windows, and I could see outside that there was another dimension of reality. I saw transparent orbs on the trees, crystalline beings, hidden folk, dancing grasses. It was like when I watched cartoons as a child, and everything in nature was happy and singing.

The mushroom people showed me a different dimension of reality that existed right in my own backyard and that I was missing because I allowed myself to get distracted by the ordinary world. There is so much more to our world than we realize. But we must open up our psychic senses to perceive the joy of life dancing around us.

Walking through the Dark Night of the Soul requires you to have your senses alive and ready to receive guidance, omens, and direction. In the dark, you'll need to be in touch with your senses to continue walking, following the flow of the river of life.

In the late 1980s, I met the Egyptian goddess Isis as a helping spirit. When I was on a vision quest, she appeared to me in a vision. She told me that she would be my ally and that she would help me bring peace and harmony back to the Earth. With the shamanic work

I teach, I lead many ceremonies for personal and planetary healing. And in every change in consciousness, we create ripples throughout the entire web of life. So, tens of thousands of people around the world have been doing ceremonies with me since I started teaching shamanism in the early 1980s.

Recently, Isis gave me a powerful message. She told me that due to all the trauma we suffer throughout our lives, we develop the behavior pattern of hypervigilance. We often are not present to what life is bringing us because we are looking around us to make sure we are safe.

When the pandemic arrived, Isis told me that people were engaging in spiritual hypervigilance. She also said that people were trying to look into the future and make predictions based upon whether they were safe or not. But she said this was a grave error because the times we live in call us to be 100 percent present. Isis also said that while looking into the future, you might miss a sign the universe put right at your feet in order to ensure your survival. If you don't stay present, you might miss it.

When we take time to immerse ourselves in the deep waters, we have the opportunity for reflecting on our own life, and we can listen to that voice within that we may not have heard on dry land. With your inner voice, you can hear unique and expanded perceptions that have been gathered during your life, through seeing a vision, hearing an important message, being given an important omen/sign of what you need to do. This voice does not come from your ego. It comes from a deep place within you, where you can feel, hear, see, taste, and smell in new ways with which you might be unfamiliar. When you hear a small voice you have quieted for years speaking the truth and touching your heart, you know you are engaging with it.

We live in a multidimensional reality. I find that many people today prefer to ride the surface waves of life and not go too deep. But, just like the treasures that Octopus finds when it is in the depth of the ocean, going deep can bring changes to your entire presence and way of being in this world. Going deep can bring you to a place where you can access your profound wisdom, the intuition you were born with, and live a life that has flow and meaning.

This, for me, all goes back to the gliding creatures of the deep sea who live alone or in small communities and are completely present in life. You might find yourself entering a flow that leads you to a life of inner peace when you access this energy.

After a female octopus gives birth, she dies, reminding us that nature is always destroying and creating, as one spiraling, flowing process.

Practice

Some of you who are reading this chapter about Octopus already have good practices to awaken your psychic senses. However, for some, this is new to you.

In shamanic cultures, initiations were used to open the third eye as well as clairaudient and clairsentient abilities.

When I was about seven or a little younger, I had a severe case of the measles and had to be blindfolded to make sure no light got into my eyes during my healing process. If light had gotten into my eyes, I would have gone blind.

As in shamanic cultures, where initiates were placed in dark caves, this would have been seen as an initiation. Living in darkness changes the brain and awakens the gift of clairvoyance, something that was very important to the survival of a community. The same was true with the ability to hear messages from the spirits, plants, trees, elements, and so on. Initiations awakened the ability to feel in the body that something was coming, something that needed to be attended to.

In addition, people in shamanic cultures who successfully completed these tough initiations created by their elders returned to the community with strength of spirit, the same strength of spirit the sea creatures and our beloved wild animals reflect to us.

One of the best ways to expand our perception is to spend time in nature and befriend a plant, tree, rock, crystal, bush, and so on. Ask, "May I step into your field of energy?" In this way, you will receive permission to approach and to relate.

Focus your eyes so that your gaze is only on the being you are relating with. Sit in meditation with it for at least twenty minutes, and don't allow yourself to become distracted. As you do this, you will notice your sense of self changing a bit. Maybe by keeping your gaze steady, you will start to feel a bit altered. You will start to notice aspects of the sacred nature being you are encountering that you have never noticed before. You might start to hear a message from it that is beyond your ordinary ears. This message might be so profound for you.

Over time, tell the nature being about yourself and listen to its story. What is its life like? What is its family like? Plants, trees, rocks, and crystals have ancestors and family, too.

As you keep up this practice, you will hear sounds coming from nature that resemble song. You will notice nature leaving you little gifts, like a heart-shaped leaf or stone in your path.

Soon you will feel that you are more aware of messages coming from life itself. These messages are filled with guidance, inspiration, and hope. They are vital to your mental, emotional, and physical health, as they put you in harmony and flow with the magical and joyous communication constantly occurring in nature.

CHAPTER 6
Narwhal

Llyn

> After my father bought our first used car when I was five years old, we took summer day trips to New Hampshire's mountains and lakes, a welcome break from the heat and confinement of our small apartment. I vividly recall the musty, earthy smell of the lake water on sweltering days, the sting upon plunging into chilled waters, and the curious sounds and sensations of being underwater.

Swimming in the pristine lakes of the White Mountains washed away my troubles. The adults appeared happier being by the waterside, too.

We also visited the coast. My brother and I ran through waves at the water's edge until we could bear the icy Atlantic. Then we bodysurfed until we were covered in goose bumps, fingers wrinkled like prunes and teeth chattering behind our blue puckered lips. My mother and grandmother said the ocean water would heal us. True to the women's words, any bumps and scrapes on our skin were soothed by the end of the day. After being in cold saltwater all day, I felt healed on the inside, too.

Perhaps my love for water as a child and for the Salish Sea where I now live, with Canadian Arctic waters to the north, are part of why the spirit of Narwhal calls to me so.

Narwhal is one of the rarest and most seldom seen whales in the world. For this reason and because its long straight tusk can remind us of the legendary unicorn, there are those who think Narwhal is only a creature of myth and lore.

To the Alaskan Inuit peoples, the narwhal is a very real and embodied being. The Inuit have viably hunted the elusive narwhal for thousands of years. It is as integral to their mythology as it is to their physical survival. The Inuit are nourished by the animal's organs, meat, and by its nutrient-dense fat. The animal is honored, and every part of it, including the tusk and blubber, is used for basic needs.

A large, strong, and fast-swimming mammal, the narwhal disappears for six months of the year into the far-flung waters of the polar night. It can dive up to almost a mile deep under the pack ice of the Arctic seas.

The few narwhals ever held in captivity have died within months. Narwhals flourish as part of the ocean's wildness. When removed from the mystery of their remote icy waters, these beautiful water beings die.

The human species appears driven to tame and invade what remains of nature's wildness. Yet, it is the unbound spirit of the Earth and our own instinctual nature that we long for now—and what will guide us through uncertain times.

The narwhal finds its prey through echolocation, emitting sounds at the dark ocean bottom that are reflected by nearby squid, halibut, and other fish. As it hunts and eats, the narwhal can stay under the water for a long time.

As a child, I sometimes held my breath to see how long I could stay under the water. In that reality, I felt totally cut off from the world of people above the water's surface. During childhood and in adulthood, there are likewise times that I've felt *metaphorically* under the water, separated from the surface activities of life that we all take for granted. We've all had colds or flus that have kept us in bed for a few days. If we have a chronic or serious condition, we may need to withdraw for weeks, months, or even for years. There are also periods when humanity retreats en masse, such as in being locked down during pandemics, at which times we may also be parted from our loved ones.

Underworld journeys can be terrifying, incredibly hard. They can make us feel as if we've sunk to the bottom of an unmapped sea. As groundless as they seem when we experience them, they are actually full of distinct features—just as the Arctic Ocean is a complex topography of ridges and valleys with a deep-sea floor that teems with amazing life forms.

Times of separation and challenge push us to chart new pathways, to find nourishing ways of holding ourselves to gather richness and meaning through our experiences.

Narwhal is at home in vast, secluded waters and finds food in the deep seas. We can call out to its spirit to help us find our way and to be spiritually fed through times of struggle and isolation.

I first encountered spirit allies like Narwhal when I moved from where I lived in the Hoh rain forest to a cottage on the north end of the Olympic Peninsula. I was in my late fifties, an age when most women I knew were long settled. I had no car—only my feet and a bicycle to get around with. I left not only my cherished forest behind but also my dog and a loved one. The parting was necessary . . . and it broke my heart. I felt sad, alone, and tentative. Yet, in this barren time, spiritual doorways opened to which I might not otherwise have found my way and which set me on a new path. My fear and sorrow did not go away overnight. But eventually, they did transform.

Most of us want to be happy and untroubled, enjoying the good things of life with our friends and families. Yet, life is never continuously like this. Unsettling and unexpected things happen. Some life phases are desolate. Others test us beyond measure. During such times, it helps to remember how precious life is and that we are never alone. We can ask nature to light a pathway for us in the dark. We can call upon caring allies to find the soul food we need. They can help us find meaning in our experience and the unique opportunities that each journey invites.

As we call to Narwhal, we can also call out to the spirit of the water. Every shamanic culture honors water as a living being and recognizes its power to heal, just as my mother and grandmother said that the ocean water would heal my brother and me.

I witnessed a beautiful water healing by the late Maya elder, Tata Pedro Cruz Garcia, to whom I brought groups to work with for several years by the shores of Lake Atitlán in Guatemala. One morning at dawn, I awoke from a dream that depicted a person in my group in distress. The dream was so strong that I got out of bed, quickly dressed, and went to find the woman. There she was lying on a daybed on the open terrace. Another woman, trying to help her, said she was having an asthma attack. Just then, Tata Pedro appeared and asked the woman to stand up and walk with him to the edge of the balcony.

Birdsong filled our ears as we stood looking out to mists that hovered like phantoms over the vast waters of Lake Atitlán. Tata Pedro guided the woman, who was having a hard time breathing, to turn her back to the lake and feel its healing force. Speaking softly, the elder then said:

> Hold your hands in prayer position over your heart. Feel your heart as one with the water's heart.
>
> On your next breath out, cup your hands together and bring them up to your mouth. Now, blow into your hands all the energy you don't need. Then, immediately move your hands out and then behind you on either side. Send this breath to the waters behind you. Feel the water absorb and transmute this energy.
>
> Now, with your arms behind you, feel the healing forces of the lake come into your hands. Let them be saturated with healing energy. Really feel this.
>
> On your breath in, move your hands from behind, back around, and toward your heart as you breathe these healing forces back into yourself.

Within minutes, this woman was breathing normally.

Even if we don't live near a body of water, we can vividly imagine the healing forces of water at our back as we enact this lovely practice. We may sense mystical Lake Atitlán no matter how many countries lie between us, feel a pristine lake an hour's drive away, or the power of the ocean a thousand miles away. There is no barrier to the healing magic of water.

Water can also spontaneously heal our hearts just as the lakes of the White Mountains washed away my troubles as a child.

In walking the beach one morning along the Salish Sea, I chanted from my heart to the waters and committed as I always do to bring about some good for nature. Within a short period of time, I was overcome with a feeling of love and gratitude for the waters. Arms spread open wide, I called out: "Thank you, waters! I love you, waters! You and I are one!" I felt this oneness in every part of my being.

Continuing my beach stroll, I rolled my pant legs up to my knees and stepped barefoot into the water to walk amid rocks hidden by seaweed. I quickly lost my footing on a slimy rock and fell into the sea. The freezing water and the pain of landing on a barnacled rock made me gasp. Yet, I had to laugh at sitting waist-deep in water. The water and I were one.

I wasn't badly hurt by my fall, yet I felt oddly shaken. In napping that afternoon, I dreamed my parents were with me in the room. They spoke to me with such care. With her palms, my mother began to pat on my back as if softly striking a drum. The beat reverberated through me and forced my heart to release its grief. I woke up crying.

Two years before, my parents had died within months of each other. This vision was a precious gift from the water. The dream had been so real—my mother and father were present with me in a way I had never known.

The next morning, my daughter, Sayre, gently asked if I wanted to share the vision that I'd mentioned with her. In relaying the simple story, a deep sorrow gripped me and my heart squeezed out the rest of its tears.

The water being and spirit of Narwhal invite us to honor the watery intelligence within us, letting our hidden depth of feeling rise to the surface and flow through us. Our hearts always seek healing, especially during times of loss and adversity.

Sometimes we need to cry our salty tears as if we are offering them back to the primordial mother of the sea. We cry for all that we have lost and left behind. We cry for those we love. We cry for our ancestors to find their way home. As we give voice to the tender places within, we can also raise our voices for nature. We cry for narwhals and for all the sea creatures and for those of the land and the air. We cry for our original peoples. We cry for every aspect of our world that is hurting, harmed, forgotten, or cast aside.

Grief is love. Every tear is an offering, an honoring. Our reverence gives our sorrow a place to rest its weary bones so that it can nourish new life. A natural goodness releases when we shed our tears, like the sweet scent the earth emits when trees drop their leaves to be alchemized into humus. This goodness or sweetness is death's promise of coming growth.

As most of us have not been supported to walk the unlit pathways of the heart, our feelings can feel like chasms. We may be made vulnerable in getting in touch with what we really feel; the sensations in our bodies may even overwhelm us.

The narwhal has a thick layer of blubber to help it swim in deep, cold water. As we dive deeply, we can call Narwhal to our side to show us how far we should go, how long to submerge, and how to insulate and feel protected. Just as narwhals are vocal and social among their own kind, kindred souls can offer comfort and safeguard us as we share. In turn, we can also create a haven for our loved ones to express, as my daughter did for me.

When there's no one to share with or when what we feel is too subtle for words, we can play a musical instrument, draw, paint, sing, gesture with our hands, or intuitively move our body to communicate from our deepness. Or we may simply sit or lie down in silence or in nature and invite what we feel. As we speak to the waters, trees, and other nature beings about what is deep-down inside of us, we will feel listened to and held in sacred space. We can make offerings of tobacco or cornmeal as we reflect, offering back to the living world.

As we share from our deep heart, we open a channel for the mystery to speak through us. The ancient songs of love and longing, suppressed and in hiding, are waiting to come alive again—in us and in our world. They will guide us all back home.

Narwhal is a powerful spirit ally who can guide us into the depths of what we feel to who we really are. With Narwhal, we can feel enriched and transformed as we travel through upheaval and change.

Magical as its spirit is and rare as this whale is, the narwhal is not a mythical animal. It is a living, physical sea mammal on a threatened voyage amid dwindling ice caps. The narwhal can stay underwater for a long time, yet it cannot live under the water; it must regularly surface for air.

After immersing in the deep waters of our feelings, we must come back to the surface of things, integrate, and ground what we've experienced into everyday life. Resurfacing can be like taking our first breath, being reborn. This is a time to look at what changes we want to make to keep life fresh and to honor the hungry parts of us that we've nourished. Our spirit will also be fed by giving back—to others and to nature. As we do, let us remember narwhals, all water beings, and all life on this beautiful planet.

 ## Practice

Working with the spirit of Narwhal has helped me to grieve and to heal, find the nourishment I need, and restore myself through water's transformative power. This nature being is inseparable from the vast waters that are its habitat. Through this practice, we can also merge with the oceanic field.

Lie or sit outside in a gentle place in nature where you will not be disturbed. Alternatively, create a restful space inside your home to sit or to lie. If inside, you may play calming music or recorded whale sounds.

Settle and become comfortable. Then take three deep, slow breaths. Feel your body grow heavier with each release of breath. Feel the support and love of the earth as if you sink into her loving embrace.

Now listen to the natural sounds or music in the space around you.

Narwhals are in harmony with natural sound, even the thunderous booms of their iceberg habitat. Yet they are sensitive to human-created noise in the ocean.

If you hear other noises, concentrate on nature or the music. Allow these sounds to infuse your body and heart with good energy just as the sun suffuses plants with vital forces.

As you breathe in the beautiful sound frequencies, also feel them saturate every pore.

Take all the time you like.

Take another nice deep breath now, and notice what you feel. Allow any tears to surface as the sounds restore your heart's harmony.

Be gentle with yourself and take your time.

Continue listening and breathing. Simply breathe and be. Sense the natural goodness that arises as you welcome all of who you are into this tender space.

When the moment feels right, you may wish to voice your own healing sounds. You may utter spontaneous sound, a soft song, or tones.

The human body is mostly water. Sounds are magnified in water and travel faster and farther in water than through air.

Sense the healing frequencies of your voice as a soft and pure energy cleansing your inner waters, cascading through you, and permeating every watery cell.

Take time to really feel this in your body.

You may also share your voice with the planetary waters. As we are nourished by the music, nature, or whale song, we can also reverberate back our deep care.

You may tone, sing, or whisper loving intentions.

Imagine that these sounds vibrate through the earth's waters and are instantaneously received by water beings.

You may also share words of gratitude, such as "Narwhal, I feel you. You are so beautiful. Thank you for guiding me. Let me also benefit you and the water and its beings."

The spirit of Narwhal and the waters will be fed by the good energy you offer.

As you harmonize with your inner waters and vast seas and water beings, feel how this opens you to a limitless ocean of love that surrounds and holds all of life.

Rest with heart, body, and mind within this oceanic field, like a cherished child releasing into the arms of its loving mother.

When thoughts arise, simply relax and feel them release and be absorbed by the oceanic field. Rest deeply in the waters within and all around you.

If feelings or tears arise, allow the emotional currents to wash through and then beyond you as they release back into the primordial ocean.

Feel nurtured and unconditionally cared for by this watery mother.

Take all the time you like. As you relax more deeply into this vast intelligent field, you will remember—you and she are one. You need never feel alone.

When you feel complete with this practice, take time to stretch and drink some fresh water. Close your eyes as you slowly drink and feel the water touch every part of you. Later or the next day, offer a prayer or a song to a lake or stream, to the rain or to the sea. Take along a trusted friend with whom you can share your deep heart. If you can't go outside, fill a freshly cleaned ceramic or wooden bowl with water and pour into it your heart's sweetest sound. Offer the water to the earth or to a houseplant.

As you move back into daily life rhythms, reflect on how you can stay connected to the oceanic field. Also think about how you can give back to water and aquatic life. One example is to give your time or money to efforts aimed at reducing anthropogenic noise in marine environments.

In offering from the heart, the richness expands.

As the waves of life crash all around, the spirit of Narwhal is a sensitive guide. In giving back to nature and harmonizing with the oceanic field, may we all move fluidly through change.

CHAPTER 7

Bobcat

Sandra

During one hot high-desert summer, I was sitting in my living room, a passive solar living room. It's the only passive solar room in our house, with big, tall windows that go from the floor almost up to the ceiling.

We feed birds, and we have lots of squirrels that we really love. Foxes come up to the bird feeder. We have a bear which we love. The bear causes a lot of problems, especially during the summer and the fall. If we don't take our bird feeders in at night, the bear will tear them down.

We also have bobcats. Bobcats, with their graceful body; short, pointed ears; and stubby, "bobbed" tail are such amazing creatures. Bobcats are gorgeous beings. As I am a cat lover, I can imagine snuggling up to a bobcat in front of a fire on a cold night. They seem like they would be so soft and their fur so warm. But, as with all wild creatures, they are not as cuddly as one would like to hope or imagine.

Bobcats are a medium-size animal and often have to fight coyotes for territory. They are highly adaptable and can live in the desert, at the edge of cities, in forests, and even in swampland environments. Like most cats, they tend to be solitary and very territorial. They mark their territory using urine, feces, and even claw marks.

Once, I was teaching an online course, and right outside my office window were two bobcat cubs playing with each other. To have watched this amazing sight has been one of the highlights of my life.

I don't have a lot of free time, but every second that I do have, I sit down in my living room to see what's happening with all the animals outside. I go into a deep meditative state where the whole world disappears and I'm just surrounded by the beauty and the wonder of nature and of the amazing creatures who come to visit our house due to how much we feed them and because we always have a water source for them.

So here I was one summer, sitting in my living room. The weather was perfect. There was no wind. Just stillness, and the sun shining brightly. Suddenly, there was a whirlwind of dust. I live in Santa Fe, and during the spring and summer, when the winds really come up, it is very dusty. There was just dust flying everywhere. I couldn't even see what was happening. Finally, after what seemed like forever, the dust cleared just enough for me to see a bobcat with a baby gopher in its mouth. All I can say is that I went into a state of shock. I've never witnessed anything like that before. This bobcat came charging with such a speed, grabbing this little gopher, and immediately carrying it off in its mouth. With the gopher still in its mouth, it walked serenely down the path, like it did not care who was around or who witnessed it in action.

The next day, I decided to perform a shamanic journey to see what this incredible omen might mean as a possible message for me. I have embraced the practice of working with omens since the 1980s, and I find that the universe is always giving us messages by providing clues from the behavior of nature beings that cross our path.

I had a very powerful journey in which my helping spirits took me back to that scene of the bobcat racing to capture the gopher. They showed me that when the bobcat was hunting down the gopher, the bobcat was just pure life force. Just pure life force was pushing this bobcat. The bobcat wasn't thinking "I'm hungry. I'd like to get a gopher." It was just pure energetic life force.

I grew up in the city, and although I've been in Santa Fe for close to forty years, I still have my city understanding of things. I didn't grow up around a lot of wild animals. I didn't understand until I had my journey and the explanation of my helping spirits what life force really was. The journey brought me back to the bobcat and the gopher and showed me the energy pouring out of the bobcat at the time. The spirits showed me the unbridled energy moving through this bobcat. In the journey, they also showed me all the unbridled energy moving through me. It was amazing. In all my years, I've never thought about life force and what life force really is.

Before we move on, I just want to give a brief definition of soul, spirit, and life force.

"Soul" is our life essence. It's that part of ourselves that keeps us alive. Our soul was looking down on this Earth, considering the possibility of taking on a life form. Earth is so beautiful, and there are so many experiences here that spirits don't get to encounter. Spirits don't get to smell the gorgeous fragrances we have here on Earth, for example, such as the smell of a rose. On Earth, we live in one community, interconnected with the web of life, sharing life energies with trees, plants, and all the beings that live in the air, water, and earth who can communicate with us and with whom we can develop a sacred relationship. Spirits don't get to touch the amazing textures we can run our hands through. They don't get to see all the amazing colors or listen to the sounds of rain, of children laughing, and so on. I always joke that many of us came here to be able to taste chocolate. Spirits don't get to taste.

Recently, I was gifted an amazing vision in which I was told that humans truly incarnated in order to touch other people's heartbeats— an experience spirits miss.

We are living in Earth-school, where we get to live out our destiny and receive the lessons we made contracts to experience before we were born. Our soul holds the passion for life, and we knew before we were born what we wanted to manifest during our lifetime.

Once we are born, our parents, figures of authority, and society all project onto us their perceptions as to how we are perceived and what our talents are in the world. We are asked to behave in certain ways instead of being encouraged to fully express our souls.

Our soul holds the knowledge of why we chose to incarnate and also decides when it is time for us to leave this great Earth. Our soul has passion for life and knows what brings passion and joy into our life. But our soul is also evolving; and due to the lessons that we must learn, our soul goes through traumas that might cause soul loss, where the soul temporarily leaves the body in order to survive an experience of post-traumatic stress disorder (PTSD). When we get abused, we suffer soul loss. Our soul flees to another dimension of reality, waiting until it is safe to come home or to be brought back home by the intervention of a shamanic practitioner. Our soul goes away to another place because it doesn't feel safe in our body. When this happens, we are suffering what's called partial soul loss. If you lose your entire soul, that's when you die. Soul loss occurs so that we don't feel the full impact of pain. It is a survival mechanism that helps us when we suffer trauma and go into shock.

The soul learns. It grows. It experiences life, and it chooses when it wants to be born. It chooses when it wants to die. When clients come to me asking about the timing of their death, I always share that it is up to your soul, not up to your ego, as to when. It's our soul that makes those kinds of choices.

"Spirit" is a reflection of Creator and the creative forces of the universe. We are the light of the Creator. You can't hurt Creator, and you can't hurt the creative forces of the universe. Nothing can hurt your spirit. It's always perfect. It's always divine. It's always light. It's always shining in you.

Your spirit is the divine part of you. We hide our light behind our mental chatter and our false egoic needs and beliefs. But in reality, when we allow our presence to fully shine, we not only heal the collective of life, but we also continue to grow, evolve, and heal from our own past wounds.

When we walk through the Dark Night of the Soul and experience our life unraveling, that is the time for our spirit to show its strength and carry us through whatever challenge we are presented with, because the point of an initiation is to polish us like a beautiful precious gemstone.

We came here to grow and evolve, and by going through traumas of the soul, our life can seem like it is falling apart. But we are just evolving into a person who has more of a presence in the world, a person who has light shining in their eyes and uplifts all of life by shining their beauty into the world.

Although we don't understand or enjoy the challenges to the growth of our soul, it is one reason that we came here. To walk out of the darkness and into a dimension filled with light, we must access that light within ourselves. And that is the strength of our spirit, the quality that gets us through the tough initiations of life so we can live like a polished stone, in harmony with all of life. In this state, we also change the world through our presence—the feminine model of healing that teaches it is who you become that heals the world.

I have been teaching and writing about soul and spirit for over forty years. But I never thought about or considered our primal nature, which is life force. Our life force is primal like that of Bobcat and every other living creature on Earth. Life force is beautiful. When my helping spirits showed me what my own life force looked like, I could not believe it. It was like a blue flame flowing through my body. It was such a magnificent moment to be able to experience my own life force. There are great lessons in moving with the flow of this energy.

A modern-day example of life force would be someone acting with superhuman strength to survive a trauma. Their body just goes on automatic mode, and the force needed to survive takes over. For example, you hear about people being able to lift extremely heavy objects to help someone in physical danger or to avoid danger themselves.

A colleague of mine relates life force to *chi* or *prana*. She remarked when reading my chapter that when Bobcat became life force, nothing else existed. This could have been true to indigenous hunters as well as hunters today who become completely at one with their life force and don't have to focus on finding prey. They immediately kill their prey in the same time as it would take a bobcat to snatch up its meal. There is no time to think, just to act.

I was climbing Mount Shasta once when what seemed to be about an eight-ton boulder headed at lightning speed down the mountain, right toward me. It almost seemed to have its "radar" on me. If I jumped right, the boulder jumped right. If I went left, the boulder went left. To get out of the boulder's path, I jumped so high that my crampons got caught in the upper part of my jacket, which seemed like an impossible move. Crampons are shoes that have cleats in them for climbing up ice. So, for my crampons to get stuck close to my shoulder was an impossible act of pure life force—signifying that I had jumped out of the way of the boulder and moved at a speed I normally would not have the ability to achieve.

People at base camp were watching all of this and could not believe what they were seeing. They had never witnessed a person jump so high to try and escape danger. In the end, the boulder missed me by about five feet. I have no recollection of jumping so high to get away from the boulder. My life force just took over.

When we need help, our life force can just take over and move us out of harm's way.

 ## Practice

As I shared, when I met my life force, I was truly astounded by its beauty and its power. The experience answered so many questions for me about people's energy and how sometimes we are tapped into such a primal aspect of ourselves that we act just as any wild creature would act to find food or fight for survival.

To meet your life force, you must get into a meditative state. If you are trained in the practice of shamanic journeying, you can work in partnership with your helping spirits. But whether you have a formal practice of journeying or not, there are an abundance of allies who can help us obtain spiritual insights and guidance.

When we are walking in darkness, we have the elements—earth, wind, water, and fire—watching out for us. And they can lead us to the answers we are seeking. First, ask for their help and then watch for the omens they show us. Reach out to others. The light of the Moon gives us guidance in our lives and while we are walking through our initiatory journey into the dark. The same is true for the Sun. The Sun teaches us about unconditional giving; it shares its light with the food that we eat each day. It is a helping spirit to anyone who asks for its guidance.

Listen to spiritual music that does not have words. First, try calling for a helping spirit who can assist you in envisioning the beauty and primal power of your life force. If a helping spirit does not show up, call on a nature being you love, such as the Sun, the Moon, or one of the elements as embodied in the Ocean, the Wind, Fire burning in a fire pit, or the Earth beneath a tree or even a houseplant.

You can just sit with an element in nature and see what information comes when you hold a strong intention of wanting to meet your life force.

You can perform this work outside in nature. A powerful way to journey is to lie on the earth, connecting with her heartbeat. Earth is 4.6 billion years old. Imagine that life force energy connected with yours while lying on such an ancient breathing being.

Absorbing the lessons of the Sun can teach you about your own life force, as the sun is the most powerful teacher we have on how to strengthen our life force. It is always feeding us with energy as it shines light for us to receive into our bodies. You can also hold your intention to meet your life force and observe what happens. You might receive an image or a feeling of your life force moving passionately through every cell of your body. You might hear a sound, smell a fragrance, feel a texture.

Try to get some idea of what your life force looks and feels like.

You can even watch videos of wild animals in nature and watch their primal life force taking over their actions.

After you receive this information, it is a powerful action to draw what you received in your journey or meditation.

And a powerful way to end this work is to dance your life force.

When I witnessed the life force of Bobcat, it was incredibly graceful but at a speed that I had not witnessed before. My life force doesn't move that fast. It is more flowing. What is your life force like? Is it like Bobcat? Is it flowing or is it a soft energy? Dancing this journey, drumming while journeying, singing while you tap into a revelation about life force are all practices I highly recommend.

There is another part to this journey: meditative practice.

When I was shown my life force, the helping spirits had dissolved me to my skeleton self, and I could watch my blue life force flowing through me. Then the spirits joined my heart energy with my life force. The message they shared with me was that every single miracle you can think of can be created if you combine life force with your heart. They said that nothing is impossible if you combine heart and life force.

The first part of your work is to meet your life force. The second part of the work is to see if you get any guidance on combining life force with your heart.

When I shared with others about combining life force with the heart, I was told this is a foundational teaching in Taoism. Although I have always been attracted to the practice of Taoism, I never learned any of the formal practices. Taoism, like shamanism, connects us back to the river of life and its flow and with everything in nature.

I have been reflecting on an interesting message I received—that one cannot die until life force is ready to let go. I am still pondering this, but I can see the primal energy that is not connected to our minds and what we think. Life force just acts as any being in nature does. And if life force is strong, we are strong. And when it is time for it to let go, we let go and we transcend into the dimension of Source and the divine.

CHAPTER 8
Black Jaguar

Llyn

We walked silently, one behind the other, on the muddy jungle path. The air smelled like damp moss. As dusk became night, the shriek of howler monkeys gave way to the sounds of frogs, insects, and nocturnal birds and animals. After a long trek, the thick canopy lifted. We had stepped into the heart of Tikal. In the vast, moonless sky, infinite layers of stars twinkled. Dimly visible at the east end of the open space stood a massive presence, the Temple of the Great Jaguar.

Our Maya spiritual guide waited for us in the center of Tikal's Grande Plaza. Using flashlights to see, we opened a jar of honey, a bag of sugar, and flowers wrapped in newspaper. We unfastened tightly tied corn husk bundles that held copal, rosemary, frankincense, chocolate, cigars, and other offerings. Sweet and woody scents escaped into the night air.

Don Fifildo wiped the earthen ceremonial platform, then he spit sacred alcohol to spiritually cleanse the space. Next, he poured from the bag of white sugar, drawing a circle then the Maya cross, equally dividing the circle into four quadrants. Flowers were strewn around the circle, small candles piled at each direction—red for the Fire Jaguar to the east, black for the Earth Jaguar residing in the west, yellow for the south and Water Jaguar, and white for the Wind Jaguar to the north.

A chill ran up my spine as we invoked the "Balam" Jaguar teachers of the four directions, starry emissaries who brought secret knowledge to guide the Maya through chaos and change. I imagined a black jaguar watching us from the dense jungle as flames consumed the fragrant offerings, the jaguar temple looming.

It is little wonder that a large feline, native to these lands and wielding immense power, holds such importance for the diverse ethnicities known as the Maya peoples, who have protected their sacred wisdom through profound challenges.

Solitary creatures who roam over large territories of land, jaguars are brawnier and slightly smaller than leopards, yet their jaw is twice as powerful as a lion's. The black jaguar represents only 6 to 10 percent of all jaguars. It lives in the densest part of the jungle that receives very little sunlight. Black jaguars see better in darkness than in the light.

We may live thousands of miles from the tropical jungles of Central or South America where jaguars live and the jaguar energies are honored, yet the Black Jaguar spirit is available wherever we are. With nocturnal vision, strength, and stealth, it offers a solid footing through change.

Although they are adept runners, black jaguars don't chase down their prey. They stalk them on the ground in the dark and make a quick kill by crushing the skull with one bite of their powerful jaws.

When life goes terribly wrong, Black Jaguar medicine cuts through panic and confusion. It is a fierce guardian of the heart and mind.

The weeks of writing this chapter coincided with heart-wrenching tragedies and the threat of world war. Shock, dread, and grief had my stomach in knots. I couldn't sleep. Black Jaguar, with its strong muscular body and laser focus, was a solid presence. I asked this ally of the darkest of forests for courage.

When nothing makes sense, and we are forced to find a place inside of us to accept the madness of the world, confident Jaguar energy ensures that we do not get lost in chaos.

You may like to try this Jaguar practice that helps me so much when I feel anguish, terror, or anger about situations I am helpless to change.

Lie on your back on a comfortable mat or on your bed, and close your eyes.

Invoke the compassionate presence of Jaguar. You may like to imagine yourself in a jaguar body.

Now, count as you take 108 gentle, steady breaths.

Focus your mind on counting and feeling each breath in your body.

Take full and relaxed breaths, not breathing too deeply or too fast.

Let your belly muscles relax as you breathe into your whole body.

Take your time. Allow spontaneous yawns or subtle movements that release energy and tension.

If you get caught in thinking, gently come back to counting the breaths. If you have strong feelings, don't push them down. Breathe with what you feel, and you will find your way through your feelings. Keep focusing on your breath and bodily sensations.

Feel your Jaguar strength.

The black jaguar is strong and agile, though it spends almost half the day sleeping and a lot of time stretching.

At 108 breaths, stretch widely yet gently. Sense how your Jaguar body wants to move to transform the held places inside. Indulge in big yawns.

Feel the Jaguar power.

Then let your movement rest, and take a deeply nourishing breath. If you want to sleep, you may enjoy imagining yourself as a heavy, totally relaxed, slumbering Jaguar body swaddled in a luxurious coat of midnight-black fur.

You can do this practice before falling asleep, if you wake up trembling in the middle of the night, before getting out of bed in the morning, or at any dedicated time. Done daily, you'll find relief from everyday stressors. The challenges may still be there. Yet each time you breathe and move, strength will flood in. Peace and perspective will grow. You'll feel greater flexibility to deal with whatever is happening.

On a spiritual level, the inner harmony we cultivate extends goodness to our troubled world.

Black Jaguar acts decisively from a relaxed state. Its medicine helps us settle our reactions and stay focused.

In the spring of 2020, I was in Guatemala facilitating a journey to work with Maya spiritual guides. The novel coronavirus had just broken into the United States.

Reorienting to the outside world in the last forty-eight hours of the life-shifting journey was jarring. The world was amok. I worried about how my trip participants would handle this. How were their families? How did they feel about returning to chaos? Would it be difficult for them to get home?

Luckily, everyone was strong and clear. Steeped in Jaguar energy and the sacred fires we had been working with, every person was grateful despite everything that was happening. They walked with power, ready for whatever we stepped into back home. Soon after every person in my group flew out of the country, Guatemala closed its borders. My own return flight home was cancelled.

My hands were shaking when I shared my predicament with my family. I got off the phone, lay on my bed, closed my eyes, and took some deep breaths. My body shuddered. I finally relaxed. In those calmer moments, I saw with my inner vision a path of light stretched a great distance before me.

A voice said, "There is a pathway through this. Feel your feet upon the path."

With its stealth, patience, and night vision, Black Jaguar helps us follow our instincts and the life force itself to find our way through the dark.

I moved from the expensive hotel where I had been staying to an affordable guest house nearby. The bustling center of Antigua was a ghost town. My knees felt weak as I walked on the cobbled streets, but I envisioned the Jaguar pathway of light and set my feet firmly upon it.

I remembered when Quechua shamans from Ecuador visited my family in the United States many years ago and we performed a fire ceremony on a beach in Rye, New Hampshire. The moon was full. Don Esteban Tamayo had the ninety group members stand in line. We all faced the ocean. Salty breezes stung our nostrils and lips. Waves crashed on the shore, and the chilled mist wetted our cheeks. The moon loomed over the Atlantic. A broad, brilliant path of light extended from the moon at the water's horizon all the way to the shore, just ahead of us.

With great feeling, Don Esteban spoke in indigenous dialect. Translated from Quechua, to Spanish, to English, he shared: "The shaman's path is a path of light with darkness on either side. The shaman must walk this path of light—and help others walk upon it. I have always seen the shaman's path with my inner vision. This is the first time in my life that I have seen it with my physical eyes."

When I arrived, the guest house host asked what brought me to Guatemala. I told him about my work with Maya elders.

"Oh," Blake said, grinning. "That's a sign, as Carlos Barrios is staying here."

I had visited Guatemala for the first time with Gerardo Barrios, Carlos's brother. The Barrios brothers were legendary experts on the Sacred Maya Calendar, and Carlos's *The Book of Destiny* was widely known. Though I'd known of Don Carlos for many years, we had never met.

I inhaled deeply. The pathway of light shimmered as if saying, "I told you so."

Upon seeing the Maya priest that first night, we both knew we were meant to meet.

Carlos and I enjoyed many conversations before I left Guatemala on a humanitarian relief flight the next week. He gave Maya spiritual readings, led fire ceremonies, and shared teachings at the guest house.

It moved me to see the strength come into people as they immersed in the traditions of these lands.

Carlos Barrios died three months later.

The timeliest wisdom Don Carlos shared that week was to approach our pandemic isolation like the five-day period of reflection that precedes the Maya new year—a time to go deep inside and open our dreaming powers to live in greater harmony with the Earth, cosmos, and all of creation.

Carlos explained that traditional Maya peoples cleaned and even painted their homes to bring fresh energy to the new year. Many of them sat in complete darkness for five days, boarding up the doors and windows so no light could come in. They reflected carefully on who they were and who they desired to be, how they could better fulfill their spiritual purpose.

This time of solitude and purification is called *Wayeb'* by the Yucatec Maya. It is known as *Tz'apil* in the Maya K'iche' language.

Maya spiritual guide Lina Barrios describes it this way: "*Tz'apil* means closing a door, for it is closing the door to the old year and receiving the new one cleansed on all levels to achieve happiness."

The great challenges we experience have been predicted by many indigenous groups. When John Perkins and I met with Hopi elders at the beginning of this century, many had stopped traveling. Foreseeing upheaval and travel moratoriums, they stayed close to their sacred lands.

Just as the door to each past year closes, the door to our collective reality—the familiar ways we have known ourselves and our world—has closed. We cannot turn around and walk back through that door. Tender and openhearted, we stand at a threshold, in the gap between what was and what is possible. This is a time to remember who we want to be and to offer the gifts we were born to share to benefit all life.

From certain angles and casts of light, the rosette designs on the blue or purple skin of the black jaguar are seen through the black sheen of its coat. This speaks to the strong yet tender heart of the warrior, inviting us to reflect on how we use power—how we can shift away from dominating cultural values to embrace an empowerment that nourishes all peoples, nature, and life forms.

Like the light that reveals the black jaguar's skin through its fur, shining the spiritual light of ceremony on the mystery of the universe opens hidden dimensions of love and beauty that are always there for us, even when we don't see or feel this to be true. It also extends good energy beyond us.

A simple—yet exquisite—ceremony you can do when your heart is heavy with the pain of the world is to create a beautiful nature object to offer to the land or waters. It's wonderful to gather with friends, neighbors, and children to do this ritual.

The Earth nurtures all of life and is plentiful in beauty. Humans find joy and come into balance with our Earth Mother when we offer beauty back to her. This good energy also reverberates out, and through our intent, we can direct love, healing, goodness, comfort, and harmony to people and events and to distant locations.

When enacting this ceremony with a group, you may want to make one creation that you can all work on together. Simply wander in nature and collect items to fashion into an artform or a wreath. Speak your good sentiments as you collect, then thank each item that calls to you, such as fallen branches, pinecones, leaves, or vines. You can make offerings to the earth, such as tobacco, as you wander. Flowers may want to be part of your creation. When I create my object, I sit outside on a wool mat on the ground, but some people prefer to take the items home with them to fashion into nature art inside. Focus your wishes as you shape your creation. Infuse it with your intentions to benefit places on the Earth that are in need and to send good energy to those who suffer.

Jaguars love to be by rivers, and they adeptly climb trees. You may choose to offer the completed creation to a river or a lake, or you could place it on a branch or exposed tree roots.

Design a simple ritual for the release.

If you have cocreated one item, invite one person to make the offering for the group. Be sure to pass the nature object to each person before releasing it, so that they may speak their heart or sing a final blessing to the Earth and to those it has been created for.

As the artform or wreath is being placed, ask everyone to envision love and beauty radiating to the Earth, waters, and to the people and events you crafted it for. Their petitions for healing, peace, goodness, and harmony will continue to emanate blessings and saturate the lands and waters long after your ceremony.

As you offer the beautiful nature creation that is full of loving wishes, feel love and beauty flood right back into you. Feel the strength and power of your open, radiant, and loving heart.

With amazing capacity to forge through the underbrush and to survive alone in the jungle, Black Jaguar conveys a deep coherence with the earth. This ally that can see better in darkness than in light helps us see from the heart to be all that we are meant to be, to walk the path of light.

There is a pathway through this. Feel your feet upon the path.

Practice

Sacred offering bundles are opened in preparation for the Maya fire ceremony, a practice dating back 12,500 years. The string that ties the bundles is never cut with a knife or scissors, as it must be untied by hand. As we unfasten the bundles, Maya spiritual guides encourage us to imagine that we unknot what's bound within us.

Below is a simple unknotting ceremony to seed good dreams for us and all earthly life.

Gather a piece of unused natural fiber cloth of about a square foot, four to eight ten-inch pieces of cotton string or yarn, four palm-sized cleansed stones, and a small bag of sesame seeds.

Just as traditional Maya did their new year reflection in the darkness, choose a quiet and dimly lit place in your home or go outside to sit where you will dream new dreams.

When you've chosen your spot, sit and envision yourself at the center of a sparkling sphere of light. Feel the presence, power, and indestructible quality of this light as you place the stones at the four Jaguar directions in the circle. Honor the earth below and heavens above, the four colors of corn, all races of people, and all visible and not visible beings in the sacred circle of life.

Feel the presence of Black Jaguar, who lives in the densest forests and spends half the day sleeping. Feel this ally's loving intention. Open to its dreaming powers. Feel the Jaguar life force, the power of the elements.

Hold the bag of seeds in your palms. Close your eyes. Reflect on the person you wish to be.

Consider carefully. Call in the most resonant vision of "you."

Why are you here? What gifts do you bring?

Black Jaguar tells us it is time to manifest our most heartfelt wishes, including many we had forgotten, as we remember we are the dreamers, imagining ourselves back to what truly nourishes all life on this planet and reconnects us with cosmic grace.

What rings true in your heart and body?

Reflect until you feel clear. See images of what life would be if these dreams were real.

Feel these in your heart and body as if you are now the person you wish to be.

Warm sensations may flood your heart. Allow good feelings to spread from your heart to every part of you.

Take time to feel what it's like to be who you are meant to be.

Spread the cloth on the floor before you. Pour a small pile of the sesame seeds into the center of the cloth.

Take a deep breath in. On the outbreath, blow the good energy of your dream into the seeds, propelling this feeling from your heart.

Infuse the seeds with your Jaguar breath three times.

Carefully wrap the cloth so the seeds won't spill out when you tie the bundle.

Take the pieces of string or yarn and tie these one by one to secure the bundle, the cloth that holds the seeds. Concentrate on the dreams the seeds hold.

Meditate with the tied bundle for as long as feels right. Feel the life glow of your dreams for you and all life.

Move into the next part of the ritual or leave the bundle to sit in the illumined circle or on the earth overnight. Alternatively, you could place it on a windowsill to be infused by moon and starlight.

When the time is ripe, hold the seed bundle as you sit at the center of the sacred circle.

Consider what prevents you from being in harmony with the Earth, cosmos, and all of creation.

What ways of seeing and behaving hold you back? What's knotted inside?

Take your time. Commit to change.

When you are clear, focus to unfasten the knots that tie the bundle. As you undo the ties, feel what's bound inside of you unravel.

Untie slowly with care, patience, and attention. It takes time, love, and understanding to untie knots that bind our world, those that cause suffering and separation.

Any unwanted energy releasing from you, or from the string or yarn, is spontaneously absorbed by the luminous sphere, shape-shifted into pure life force energy. This energy adds more vibrance to the seeds and to your dreams.

When you have untied the final knot, leave the string in a small pile. Take the bag of sesame seeds out on the land to scatter and offer them.

You can create a simple ceremony on your own for this action. As you offer the seeds, feel the earth take in the nourishment of the good dreams you infused them with. Feel the earth help you ground them into this reality, amplifying their power.

Take all the time you like.

To close this ceremony, return to sit in the circle of light. Commit to manifest your dreams. Thank all beings you invited into the circle. Thank Black Jaguar. Feel these release and dissolve into the luminous sphere.

Now, feel the sparkling ball of light condense until it becomes one with the fabric of your body. Feel your open and loving heart, your radiant presence.

The string has no residual energy—it is neutral. It and the cloth can be offered to a ceremonial fire or be buried in the earth. As you do so, envision the life shifts you will make to honor and manifest your dreams. Feel the earth or the fire empower these. Some people like to move like a jaguar to embody the strength and focus to bridge their dreams into this reality.

Thank the earth and thank the fire.

Feel free to adjust these instructions in ways that call to you. You may want to perform the entire ceremony by a ceremonial fire and offer the seeds to the fire. You may want to gather people together for the ceremony. Follow your heart, asking Black Jaguar to guide you.

I have never seen a black jaguar. Yet I've hiked in the Oriente of Ecuador, the Maya Forest of Guatemala, the Selva Lacandona in Mexico, and the Tumbes-Chocó-Magdalena region of Panama, where jaguars live. These tropical rain forests are exquisitely beautiful and rich in biodiversity. Yet habitat loss is the black jaguar's main threat. The forests are rapidly shrinking. As we dream good dreams, let us also help efforts to preserve the biospheres of these powerful and mystical beings.

CHAPTER 9
Pine and Juniper Trees

Sandra

As I have shared, the landscape I live in is filled with juniper, pinyon pine, and ponderosa pine trees. They have the most magnificent fragrance. It does not matter which season cycles around—the trees always stay green. So, I love to sit and have tea or a meal while staring out of my windows at the beautiful greenery surrounding my living space. It is such an honor to live here.

In my years of dealing with a health issue, I spent so much time on my couch or in bed, going back and forth to look out the windows and just nurture myself in the power and magic of this community of trees that I have such a deep relationship with.

Many years ago, Santa Fe went into a serious drought, and we lost more than six million pinyon pine trees in New Mexico due to an infestation of the bark beetle. My husband and I could not give the trees the water they so desperately needed. But we could greet every tree and share our love. We could see the trees thriving in their divine light, being fed by the sun.

Our loving actions showed us the power of love in the midst of a disaster, as we hardly lost any trees and our trees remained healthy.

While I was so ill, I really could not walk more than the distance from my house to the car. But as soon as I got the strength to walk longer distances, I immersed myself in the smell of the pinyon and juniper trees around our house and in our arroyo.

A very popular practice today is called *Shinrin-yoku*, Japanese for "forest bathing." To forest bathe means to derive great healing and relaxation from life's stresses by spending time walking among the trees, which put out a variety of compounds called *terpenes*, said to have a variety of health benefits. Much has been written on this powerful healing practice through which we can connect so deeply with nature, helping us move back into harmony with it.

Terpenes are the compounds that give trees and plants their fragrances. These fragrances on their own can relax us, take away our pain, bring us to a sense of peace, and have many positive effects on our body.

I often daydream about going to Japan to do some forest bathing. But my husband keeps reminding me that we can do our own forest bathing at our house, and we do.

I burn herbs that grow on our land to be able to truly inhale the smell. I especially like to burn pinyon and juniper needles, which make wonderful smudge sticks. These sticks are a way to tie herbs together to easily use them like incense.

In parts of the Middle East, juniper smoke is how the shamans enter into non-ordinary reality, as the smell of the smoke alters their consciousness.

I burn pinyon and juniper to cleanse myself energetically, to connect with the land and my own spiritual practices, and also to provide healing to my brain by smelling the fragrant smoke. It is a known fact that the brain loves fragrances. As I do this, I imagine the magic of the trees on my land sharing their healing with me.

Both pinyon pines and junipers have an amazing ability to survive challenging climates. Juniper trees can send their roots thirty feet into the earth for water. And juniper and pine trees have been used in Central Asian cultures to create Prayer Trees. These trees volunteered themselves to hold people's prayers and take them to the creative forces of the universe. There is a very long tradition of a shaman finding a juniper tree that is willing to be a Prayer Tree for the people. And then days and days of ceremonies are performed to create a link between humans, the tree, and the divine. Multicolored ribbons are placed very loosely on the branches in order to not harm the tree. These ribbons hold the deep emotion from the people in the community who have prayers for themselves, each other, and for the planet.

Outside my bedroom, I have a Prayer Tree that I worked with in ceremony to agree to accept prayers from me and those on whose behalf I put ribbons. This juniper tree is so ancient. I did not pick a young juniper tree with branches that look new and healthy. I picked a tree that has weathered so many storms and has initiation stories like me. We are very bonded, and I love placing prayers on the branches for myself, clients, students, loved ones, the helping ancestors of the land, the spirit of Santa Fe, the Hidden Folk, earth, air, water, and fire, and all the creatures that inhabit the elements.

But before I had this glorious ancient juniper tree to work with, I did all my ritual and ceremonial work at a beautiful pinyon pine tree that stood so proudly next to our bird feeders, not far from my living room window. This was my ceremonial tree with which I did every solstice and equinox ceremony, every ceremony before I taught, saw clients, or traveled. It was the tree I honored—I knew that the tree was a perfect bridge between heaven and earth. I always ended all my ceremonies at this tree with "May the work of the mother and father be done!"

I so loved—and still love—this tree. And I worked with it in ceremony for more than twenty-seven years. Then the most amazing event happened, which is sad but also heartwarming.

I was teaching a teleconferencing class one night in my office. The class went very well, and I enjoyed the session very much. Nothing out of the ordinary seemed to happen. I put down the phone and stood up, and I felt something like a huge jolt of lightning surge through me. I had literally been struck by lightning as a child, so I still remembered what it felt like.

I lost my balance and started to pass out. I caught myself and held on to a wall. I told my husband the class went well, but I was tired and going to bed. I figured whatever I was experiencing would just wear off in the morning.

The next day I felt so strange, but I could not explain how I felt. I wanted to go to the ER, but what would I say? "I feel the worst I ever felt in my life, but I can't tell you any more than that."

So, I stayed home and tried to rest. Shortly after that, I noticed that my head was a little pointed to the right instead of straight. My husband could not notice the shift in my head. I went to my chiropractor, and he could not see it either. But I was very aware of a change. I just was not aware of how this change would interrupt my life for so many years.

I went to California to teach, and my head remained pointed to the right. I literally had to hold my head to look straight. I had no idea

I had developed an extremely rare brain disorder that is a movement disorder. My brain had been traumatized. The neurologists I went to felt that it was a buildup of too much stress in my life. I took care of my parents for years before they died, then immediately wrote two books, and then started teaching very large online classes. I had to spend an amazing number of hours on the computer.

I have always loved to be in service. Even as a child, people would stop me on the street to tell me their problems. I started working in my father's retail store at the age of seven. Some customers would tell me they only came in to talk to me. So, I have always had this love for helping people, nature, and the Earth. I just got overzealous and forgot to take care of myself. This turned out to be a very valuable teaching, as I have learned about the power of keeping boundaries and not trying to solve every problem for others.

The neurologists I saw thought I had a perfect storm that impacted my brain. The neuroscience field has been researching this disorder since the early 1900s and still doesn't know what it is or where it is in the brain. This is a severely painful condition on every level, and it is hard for me to function in life.

So much of this book was born from the journey I have been on, as this disorder brought me into a walk through the Dark Night of the Soul. I have questioned everything in life. As painful as this condition is on every level, the lessons I have learned are also exquisite.

Here is the miraculous and amazing part of this story. The day that I developed this brain disorder and my head turned right and stayed to the right, my ceremonial tree fell over in the same direction that my head went. There had been no wind. We were getting good rain, so we had enough water to keep the trees somewhat happy. And pinyon trees are strong fighters and can survive through a lot of conditions.

My husband and I hired tree specialists to come out and look at the tree. No one had an explanation. The tree looked so healthy!

After seven years of dealing with this disorder, the tree is still alive and still growing branches and pinecones.

A little less than a year ago, I felt the strong urge to buy a particular gemstone necklace. When the necklace arrived, there was a little ruby in the box. The instructions were to bury the ruby somewhere on the land as a thank-you.

It was an obvious choice for me to choose my ceremonial pinyon tree as the burial site. There is a little curve in the trunk that leaves a small opening where one can leave things in the soil under the tree.

The day after I buried the ruby under the tree, what replaced it was a perfectly heart-shaped piece of lichen. It was like someone cut it out to be a perfect heart. I was so touched. I posted photos on Facebook. I wanted the world to witness this miraculous event.

When we develop a strong relationship with nature and the nature beings we live with, there is so much love and support that is being shared, as if this being is our best friend. And so, Pinyon became an ally for me as it joined me in my journey through darkness.

And Juniper, who accepts my prayers for healing on a regular basis, connects me with the divine within and the divine without. The wind always comes while I leave a prayer on the tree. It brushes my face and then changes directions, letting me know that my prayers have made it to the power of the universe. I guess in this way, both Juniper and Wind are my allies also. Wind has always promised me it would help me and protect me.

Everything I have gone through has opened me to so many questions about life and how the universe works. Developing a crippling disorder can bring up all kinds of existential questions. And I have spent a lot of time in nature just observing what happens when some devastating event or storm "rearranges" a landscape.

This all brings me to the very important and most complex topics of when do you keep fighting, when do you surrender, and when do you accept?

Should I be fighting so hard to heal an issue that just doesn't want to seem to heal? When do I stop fighting? And when do I keep fighting?

For me, I did keep up the fight for a long time, although my helping spirits and any practitioner that worked on my behalf advised me to surrender. For me, the word *surrender* means giving up. It feels like such a disempowering term to me. And I do not even know how to take an action to surrender. Surrender, I think, comes in its inherent timing. It is not something that can be forced.

As I continued to reflect on this over the years, I came to the importance of acceptance. Acceptance creates a more positive feeling for me than surrender. Surrender to me feels like I have no power. It is true that sometimes during a walk through the Dark Night of the Soul, you have no power or no control. Metaphorically speaking, there are times in which you do have to raise the white flag, saying, "I surrender." You can ask, "What does the universe want from me? Give me an omen. Give me a sign so I can take my next step forward." Omens, which are signs, do come during this period but always from a surprising source, not from where you expected.

For me, when I can get to a place of acceptance, I can find some peace. With acceptance, you understand that an issue is just what life brought to you to clear some karma, to grow, to evolve, and to live out your destiny. With acceptance, it still does not mean that I am happy about where life has brought me, but by accepting where I am, I can find a sense of peace.

This is such a tricky topic, as it brings up questions such as "When do you keep fighting for your health, your rights, your dreams? When do you start to reevaluate and start to move into acceptance and surrender?"

What I ended up learning for myself was that when I could move into a place of acceptance, I could find rest. And with this rest, I started to regenerate on many levels, giving me the physical, emotional, and mental energy to start fighting again to heal.

At the same time, I feel a strange state of peace, realizing that, like the pinyon tree lying on its side for the rest of its life, I might not heal.

 ## Practice

It is important for us to get an understanding for ourselves on what resistance, acceptance, and surrender mean to us. When you meet challenging situations in your life, when you start walking through the darkness, these three energies will keep morphing back and forth in your life.

There are such swings that happen in the Dark Night of the Soul, as your ego doesn't really know what the best overall action is to take in such challenging times. Your ego might say, "I won't give up." But at some point, your ego gives up and can't keep up the fight, and your inner all-knowing Spirit steps in and leads to the state of acceptance.

You might reflect on resistance, surrender, and acceptance so that you can get your own understanding for yourself. If you have a practice of shamanic journeying, you can consult with your helping spirits. You can journal, drawing images of what these three words mean to you. As you listen to some spiritual music that awakens a sense of inner knowing in your own body, you can dance the energies. You can sit or walk in nature as a time of reflection.

It's always a dance to find tools to help you move forward during challenging times. But it is good to get your own sense of what energy you are riding right now in your own life. Are you riding the energy of resistance, surrender, or acceptance?

Is the energy you are riding working for you, or do you need a change?

Again, writing can give you a lot of information. Or, if you dance, you can scan the feelings in your body. Do you feel calm, or agitated and ready to fight? Do you feel like just falling down from the stress? Where are you in your process?

As I shared, this is a tricky topic to truly understand. For one thing, we are also ruled by our karma and destiny. If you feel that this is an issue, you can always perform a ceremony in nature to break any contracts you feel are coming from a past life or from karma. You can perform a ceremony to state to the universe that you are moving into a state of acceptance.

To conduct such a ceremony, you can write down what you want to release on a piece of paper and burn it, blow your issue or belief into a stone and put it into water, or bury it in the earth to release it. Find a way to release karma or a past life event—you can even blow bubbles or run into the wind.

Always remember to ask that whatever energy you release be transformed into love and light, so that those are the energies with which you are feeding the Earth and all of life.

CHAPTER 10

White Birch Tree

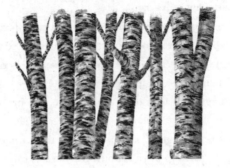

Llyn

> I arrived at a tiny Siberian village near the Altai Mountains twenty-five years ago. Snow lightly fell, and the air was sweet with the scent of wood smoke. Slender white birch trees covered the hillsides, and the paned windows of humble wooden homes exuded a warm glow. The scene was magical, as if I had walked into a dream. Stepping inside a woodworker's shop, I saw many round birch-bark boxes, like those I've seen throughout Siberia. I purchased a small round box that still sits in my home. Painted in fine detail on its surface is a snow-covered village surrounded with white birch trees.

I grew up with the luminous white birch trees of New Hampshire. The birches, with their massive white trunks that grew in front of our church, were meaningful presences for our French Canadian community.

Trees are important symbols of the spiritual life of every religion and culture. In Siberia, white birch trees are revered as the connector between the spiritual worlds. They are also known for their medicinal and shamanic powers. White birch branches were traditionally used by Siberian shamans to wash away stagnant energy as well as to spiritually cleanse individuals and their homes. Quechua people I have worked with in Ecuador also brush the body with plants in their healing ceremonials.

Anyone can cleanse the energy field with plant bundles or tree branches. This is easy to do for yourself, and it's a beautiful ritual to do with family members and friends. Children love helping to collect and work with the plants; it always seems to come naturally for them.

Just tune in to a nonpoisonous plant or tree that grows where you live. See what nature being calls to you. Then, ask its permission to remove a few sprigs or a small branch for healing. Make sure there are no thorns, hairs, or insects on stems, leaves, or needles that could irritate or enter the skin. Make sure that the nature being grows abundantly in a healthy environment and that you and anyone participating aren't allergic to it. If you sense a "no" response, thank the nature being, offer cornmeal or tobacco to the plant or tree, and move on. If you sense a "yes," make offerings to the being, ask which portion of branch or stem it offers, and hold your hand above the place where you will make the cut. Feel life force exude from your hand into the living tree or plant. Say a prayer that the cutting will not harm it. When the time feels right, release your hand, gently snip below that spot, then rest your hand again for a few moments on the cut area. Lastly, make an offering to this nature being and express your deep gratitude.

To do the cleansing, you can tie or hold the branches or plants together and sweep your body with the bundle from head to toe. You may do this fully clothed indoors, although it's ideal to feel the plants on as much of your skin that you can expose, allowing yourself to be in nature. Gently brush the plants over every part of your body, sensing any dense areas growing spacious as whatever is not needed is washed away. Take your time. Open your heart to the spirit of this tree or the plants. Sense the healing power of this plant or tree spirit flooding into and energizing every part of you as you feel the sensations on your body.

When I lived in New England, the hemlock trees, with their soft needles and beautiful spirits, made wonderful cleansing wands. In the Pacific Northwest, there are also hemlocks, as well as many ground plants that work well, such as the broad, velvety leaves of the thimble-berry plant. See what plants or tree branches call to you on or near the lands where you live.

Flick the plant bundle or branch toward the earth or toward a window out to the sky when you sense the plant is heavy with energy. The Earth and cosmos will transmute whatever is released into life force energy.

When your heart is lighter and your energy is fresher, the cleansing is complete. Place the plants on a windowsill or in the sun for a day to reenergize them so that they may be reused. Or offer them back to the earth with gratitude.

It is said that *birch* means "bright, shining one." It's easy to feel this tree is full of light when you come upon a stand of birches in the woodlands.

Two decades ago, I facilitated a daylong pilgrimage for women in the lowlands of Mount Monadnock in New Hampshire. My children, who were then twelve and fourteen, carried some of the women's daypacks. Eben and Sayre also offered a hand as we moved through rugged terrain. The women were moved by their attention and care. We had exquisite experiences immersing in nature that day includ-ing as we passed through a wood of white birches. The trees were so radiant and welcoming that we decided to ceremoniously walk one at a time through this "bridge of light" to honor the shining grove.

Several weeks after our mountain retreat, one of the women emailed us the image of a photograph she took of the bridge of light. There in the center floated a large glowing orb.

I have sat with and among White Birch and other trees since I was a young girl. The trees washed away my pain, renewed my energy and spirit. Trees are full of light and healing forces.

All plants and trees can recharge us, the land, and atmosphere. Yet, White Birch has special renewing abilities, as it restores the earth after hardship. This tree flourishes where nature has been harmed, where forests have been ravaged by fire, or where ecosystems are otherwise compromised. It grows quickly, is resistant to disease, and thrives in any soil.

Although delicate in its beauty, the white birch is resilient to harsh winters in the climates where it grows, such as New England, northern Europe, and Eurasia.

Like the White Birch, some people are naturally hardy, yet others of us may appear more fragile. No matter what our disposition, we've all felt overwhelmed at times. The spirit of Birch invites us to become familiar with what replenishes and renews our strength when we're really struggling. Just as a healthy forest is diverse, we're all unique, and our needs can also change with the circumstances.

Despite the many shamanic and spiritual practices that I do, as I am a highly sensitive person, during the most stressful times, the best medicine is usually just to *be*. I may sit in an unlit room like a tree absorbing the richness of a dark moonless night. I may listen to beautiful music or to birds singing, watch the trees swaying outside my window, or sniff the earthy aroma of a small pouch I filled with cedar and white pine tree needles many years ago. If I can go outside, I lie on a wool mat upon the earth and breathe in her energy and rich scents. As I release to nature, she gently brings me back to myself. Strength floods in.

The unique papery bark of birch trees easily peels and can fall off in long strips. I have two large sleeves of white birch bark that the land gifted me in my home state of New Hampshire many years back. These are treasured possessions, as they connect me with trees I have loved since I was a child. My childhood memories are filled with white birch trees.

The white birch that grows from the charnel grounds of a destroyed forest teaches us to gather from the ashes of our lives what will revive as well as help us grow. Just as papery birch bark can be written on, we can tap restorative wisdom by writing about or sharing experiences that have really weathered us.

The power of story is ancient. Having our story witnessed by someone who cares is healing. I recall a former colleague who didn't want to hear me repeat my account of a time I almost died, despite how profoundly this event impacted me. I could only imagine the stories this person denied within herself.

There are stories whose effect on us is so great that they become a guiding force in our lives, an ally. To respect our initiatory stories, we sensitively sift through their meaning over time.

I did my first vision quest well over ten years ago. Although I've always wanted to do another vision quest, I am still uncovering the gifts and meaning of the only formal quest I have ever done. I realize I may be mining the riches of this compelling experience for the rest of my life.

Life is a vision quest. Our stories, especially those that have changed or set us on a new path, must be steeped in to be integrated so we can be forged and strengthened by them.

Then there are times when we're just stuck in the past, repeating old stories. I know of spiritual teachers telling people to throw their story out the window, encouraging them to be present without a story-line. It's wise to leave fear and limitation behind. Yet, what I'm afraid of or was truly heartbreaking tugs at me until I touch and honor the vulnerable places inside. They carry the silver lining of my experience.

Consciously sharing the stories that beg to be heard always brings me unexpected gifts. It also makes me feel more present and alive.

It is rare to feel really listened to, yet trees do listen. In sharing deep moments with trees, the tales we unravel in their presence can nourish us.

Practice sharing your stories with a healthy living tree. White Birch, as the life form that arises from damaged lands, represents light that doesn't separate itself from darkness. It is a light that literally comes out of tragedy, which alchemizes into rich humus to support new life. As your old story is heard and held sacred by the tree, you will sense a fertile space for fresh stories to grow.

We may at times feel afraid of getting lost in our stories, absorbed by our suffering—the spirit of White Birch lifts us up to the light. It encourages a beautiful balance of acknowledging and honoring what is damaged or dying and creating beauty from it. Feel this light being lift you from saddened places as you offer your story to the tree to be transmuted.

The spirit of the White Birch is a profound teacher of death, transformation, and rebirth. It guides us through the dying times to honor what has passed and transform loss into beauty.

In the last few years, I lost my parents within five months of each other, my young adult nephew, my dear uncle, a close friend of twenty-five years, and four indigenous elders I've worked closely with. This was a lot of loss in a short period. I was sometimes overwhelmed with grief in losing those I was closest to.

When each person died, I made offerings to the Earth. I created altars for my family members. I placed on each altar a photo of my loved one, a bouquet of flowers, a beeswax candle, a bowl of water, and small food items. I offered prayers and practices for many days to help the person not cling to what is left behind, open to a wakeful journey.

The Tibetan *phowa* is among the practices I offer for those who are dying or have died. Instructions are found in *The Tibetan Book of Living and Dying* by Sogyal Rinpoche.

Just as White Birch is a luminous being that grows out of death, a small altar created with love and care is infused with beauty and light. Just as white birch trees are beautiful shining columns that arise from fields of death, spiritual practices radiate brilliance that can offer signposts in the afterlife.

Making offerings to the Earth, doing dedicated practices, and creating an altar for a loved one lift me from my dark places of loss. I remember my grief is love, a force I can direct to those I care for to help them on a light-filled journey back home to Spirit.

I have also donated to tree-planting organizations, on behalf of people who have left this Earth plane, for hundreds of trees to be planted on degraded lands. Like White Birch, who creates beauty after life is lost, as we renew and restore our lands, good energy is generated for our loved ones who have passed. Seeding new life also revives us.

There are many species of birch trees. The aspens I grew to love during the years I lived in Colorado and which always reminded me of white birch trees are not actually part of the birch family. Yet, the alders of the Pacific Northwest, whose white bark is a symbiotic organism, are related to the birch. The alder shares similar qualities, as it is one of the first trees to grow on land that's been devastated by clear-cutting. It grows quickly, fixes nitrogen in the soil, and repairs damaged lands.

Both white birch trees and alders have a life span of about forty to sixty years. Their final gift is to release their body—canopy, trunk, and roots—back to the earth to create soil and space for new trees to grow so that the forest can return.

 ## Practice

Go to a beautiful place in nature or to a park where you can wander for a time undisturbed.

If you cannot go outside, you may enact this entire practice as a guided journey experience in your imagination.

At the beginning of your wandering, sprinkle some tobacco or cornmeal on the land as you hold the intention that part of a tree will find you—such as a stick, a fallen leaf, a branch, or a twig, pinecone, or acorn.

When you feel ready, step over the spot where you made the offerings to mark your entry into sacred time and space.

Open your heart and your senses as you walk gently across the land. Notice what you see, smell, taste, and hear. Feel each movement of your body and any breezes or plants that brush against your skin. Feel gratitude for the life all around you: plants, trees, stone people, land, water, and the animals and other living forms that these lands and waters support. Feel gratitude also for the invisible ones and the spirits of these lands. Open your heart.

Remember the ancestors of these lands. Ancient trees with massive canopies may have loomed over these lands, as well as ancient waters and stone people. Feel your gratitude. Also feel your gratitude for the ancient peoples who lived on these lands, our original peoples. Open your heart to those who may have walked these lands long ago that we may not recognize. The earth's true story is full of mystery. Feel your gratitude and your proper place within the sacred circle of life.

If you live in an area where white birch trees grow, that is wonderful. Yet, all trees and plants hold the power of regeneration and renewal.

When a stick finds you (a fallen branch or twig on the ground), take a moment to connect with it while you ask if it wants to work with you. If you feel in your body and heart a "yes" response, then you may pick up the twig or branch or stick and sprinkle a small amount of tobacco or cornmeal over it as a simple cleansing and make an offering on the ground in its place.

Next, take a moment to connect with this stick, branch, or twig in whatever ways feel right to you.

What is the object's shape and color? What is the texture of its bark?

Close your eyes and sense into the spirit of the tree through this stick. What do you intuit or feel?

Take time to honor the tree or plant being connected with this branch or twig. Imagine it in your mind's eye or simply feel its presence in your heart. Feel your gratitude. The tree is a living, conscious spirit you can connect with. This humble stick holds its own and the tree and nature's energy. Respect its power to help you heal and transform.

Continue to wander, and as you move across the land, speak with this tree being through the stick or twig. Share with it your worries, fears, losses, and problems, and ask its help to honor what you feel. Share as if this is the first time, and the last time, that this story will ever be told. The tree is listening. It will absorb the authentic goodness of what you share. Take your time. Feel the old stories being respected, as their energy is also transmuted.

When you have voiced the sorrows you carry, sense the lightness, space, and regenerative qualities this tree can help you tap.

Remember how deciduous trees lose their leaves and are dormant through the cold months as if they die. They then come back to life in the spring.

Ponder how trees replenish damaged lands so new life can grow.

Feel the incredible power of trees to restore, renew, and revive life.

As you continue wandering, breathe with these restorative qualities. Ask the tree to make these come alive for you.

If you are drawn to do so, wave the nature item you hold in the air in front of your heart or around other parts of your body that call for its energy. Ask the nature form and tree spirit to which it is connected to guide you. Open your heart also to the living trees that are around you. Sense the areas in your body in which tension has built and feel them relax, renewed. Feel this space open to fresh, life-affirming stories.

Take deeply nourishing breaths, and invite revitalizing energy to fill every part of you.

When you feel complete with your experience, take time to thank the tree being that wandered with you. Make offerings to the earth. Thank all trees for their beauty and presence.

Finally, sense where this nature item would like to lie. Or whether it would like to be buried, its good energy planted in the earth. Ask the nature item what it would like. As you offer this tree being back to the earth, express your gratitude. Also ask it to extend its gifts of renewal and regeneration to the lands. Imagine this nature item radiating its blessings to the trees, stones, waters, and nature beings of these lands and to nearby lands that may be disrupted. Know that as our lands are renewed, people will also be revived.

Close your experience by retracing your steps, making offerings, and stepping back over the threshold.

CHAPTER 11
Eye of the Storm

Sandra

As I was writing this book, the collective has been experiencing quite the storm. We have been dealing with a pandemic that has stopped all of life as we know it and created an amazing amount of division among people, even between people and nature. The turbulence and the division have become so great that it feels like we are in the midst of a life-threatening and destructive storm. The pandemic itself killed millions around the world and separated families from each other. The intolerance toward those dealing with this deadly storm has caused division, which has created an even more threatening situation. And of course, all of us in our lifetime are and will be experiencing literal turbulent storms due to the environmental situation we have created on our planet.

Storms and turbulence are part of life. Through their dishonoring and unkind behavior toward all nature beings and each other, humans seem to create even more devastating storms in life. So, the question is, How do we find protection and inner peace when we enter such turbulent stormy weather? Where do we take shelter and find inner peace? And how do we hold space for each other during these times?

In this chapter, I will share with you how to find inner peace by journeying into the Eye of the Storm and how to learn to hold space for others without interfering or getting lost in dramas you have no power to fix.

I know there are places on Earth where there is calmness, because we always have balance somewhere, don't we? But a lot of us are just dealing with the turbulent waves. So, I would like to lead you on a very powerful journey. But first I would like to share a story about going into the Eye of the Storm.

In the late 1990s, I was teaching a five-day soul retrieval training in Tennessee. I had contacted a church that had a retreat center located in a beautiful landscape. I was not sure how a group practicing shamanism would blend in with the staff at the church. During the talks about our contract, I shared that we would be doing some spiritual work and we would be using drums and rattles and doing some of our work out in nature. They had absolutely no concerns about this whatsoever. Our group got along so well with all the staff.

Actually, we watched quite a lot of TV together since our workshop was taking place during the famous OJ Simpson trial. We all watched and held hands through the intensity of this trial.

The church staff did not know what soul retrieval was. I was teaching a shamanic workshop on how to bring back soul parts that get lost during emotionally, mentally, and physically traumatic events in our life. It is such a powerful cross-cultural healing practice, and in many shamanic cultures, soul loss is perceived as the most common emotional and physical illness. This ceremony has healed tens of thousands of people in our modern-day culture.

Part of the workshop included having participants practice performing soul retrievals on each other. This is always such an amazing part of the workshop, where each participant gets their lost soul parts returned to them, and they can experience for themselves the immense power of this healing ceremony.

That night, the night of our soul retrievals—of returning lost essence to our body—without having a clue what the group was doing in our circle, the staff served stuffed sole for dinner. This was such a synchronistic moment, and my group could easily find the humor in it. It showed the magical connection we had with the staff and the spirit of the land.

When I enter a retreat center to begin teaching a workshop, I always start by honoring the spirit of the land. I let the ancestral spirits of the land, as well as the spirits of the land, know that I am bringing a group of open-hearted people to the center. Although we don't know the ways of the people who have inhabited the land before our arrival, we have good hearts, a desire to be in service to all of life and to the Earth. I always ask for spiritual help and support of our work together as a circle. People travel from all over the world to be at my workshops, and we all have such a desire to heal ourselves and help others heal and evolve into caretakers of our great Earth.

As part of my workshops, I typically lead fire ceremonies to help people release an old wound into the fire or to ask for a blessing of a desire. After I greet the spirit of the land, I go to the fire pit on the land, leave offerings, and let the spirits know our intention to lead a powerful healing ceremony on the last evening of our workshop.

Well, in this workshop, we had a particular challenge. After our training began, Hurricane Opal was starting up. I was quite nervous about how we would perform our final ceremony. But I learned about the power of being in the Eye of the Storm.

The night that was intended for letting go of old hurts and pains with our important fire ceremony arrived, and I did not want to disappoint the group by canceling the fire ceremony. But the fierce winds and rain were so strong, there was no way we could work at the fire pit.

There was a little room with a fireplace that the staff said we could use. It would be a tight fit for all of us together. We would have to stand a bit as if we were on a New York subway train at rush hour, bodies leaning on each other for support.

I had chosen our fire keepers in the morning, and during dinner they went to work building a little fire for us. One of the important things I have learned over the years of conducting ceremonies is that if you enter a ceremony with the right frame of mind, it does not matter what the conditions are. By setting the right intention, all ceremonies are perfect. So, I knew our ceremony would be healing and powerful. But of course, we were all a little disappointed. The fire pit was in the most beautiful landscape, so to have had nature witness our work and hold space for us there would have been incredible.

The group had the best attitude, and the usual excitement that I was used to seeing around fire ceremonies was building during dinner.

We were starting our process of gathering outside the room, waiting for the fire keepers to invite us to be spiritually cleansed before entering our ceremonial room. At the time, I noticed something was happening outdoors. To my disbelief, the winds and rain became silent. There was perfect stillness in the air. It was like an elderly

Grandmother spirit had come through, hushing the immense sound of the wind and rain. I realized we were entering the Eye of the Storm!

I then instructed the group to go into our small ceremonial room and take wood to carry outside to the fire pit. We ran and hurried, because we had no idea how much time we would have before the hurricane returned.

In my workshops, the fire keepers typically build the fire for us and then welcome us into the circle. But since we certainly had no worries about the danger of fire on this night, the entire group worked together to build a beautiful, immense bonfire. We worked quickly to create a ceremonial fire and welcomed each other into our circle. We drummed and rattled and sang with joy as we witnessed each person's dance around the fire with a talisman they had created during the day. The talisman held the energy of the pain or memory to be released into the fire, which was to be transformed into the energy of love and light that would feed the collective of life.

The stillness in the air was palpable. It was clear we were stepping into the magical moment of being in the Eye of the Storm.

All of a sudden, when the very last person placed their talisman into the fire and I ended the ceremony by thanking the spirits for holding space for us and supporting our work, the wind began to stir and the rains returned with such a heavy downpour that we all had to run as fast as we could into the church for shelter from the storm.

The Eye of the Storm is the best place to take shelter when life becomes a turbulent storm itself. It is a place where you can be in peace, utter stillness, and find your own center. When we are going through the turbulence of a hurricane or a storm, everything gets turbulent inside us. Our emotions get stirred up. But once you can get into the Eye of the Storm, it is calm and peaceful. You can just float. I'd like you to consider the Eye of the Storm as a metaphor for a tool we can use in the Dark Night of the Soul. When we feel like we are in stormy weather in the darkness, there are practices we can perform to move into the Eye of the Storm and just rest.

Practice

I am a teacher who likes to perform ceremonies in groups. Of course, personal ceremonies are powerful. But when we join with others, we feel more connected to the power of the work. In the shamanic worldview, ceremonies and all the work we do in our practices are outside of time. This means that I can lead a group ceremony, and whenever you join in, you will have an experience of being with a group, even if it is years from now.

When I take people into the Eye of the Storm, I like to use what is called a Spirit Boat. It is a way for a group to come together and have a vehicle to take us into the magic and power of the unseen realms together. If you are willing to use the power of your imagination, you will feel yourself in a group experience.

You can listen to any spiritual music while performing this exercise. If you are willing to try this powerful guided journey, you can also drum or rattle with me as I guide you.

Before beginning, it is important to spiritually cleanse yourself so that your mind does not get in the way of the work ahead. You can use the smoke of your favorite incense to cleanse yourself. You can use a feather to clear your energy field. You can even meditate for a couple of minutes to quiet your mind. The point is that we want to move your mind out of the way so that your spirit has the freedom to move into the unseen realms without being held back by too much mental chatter. Taking a short walk in nature is another way to prepare for your work. You can also light a candle, which represents that you are calling in your spiritual power to perform this journey.

Once you have prepared, find a comfortable place to work, and put on some music or find a musical instrument to use so you can be more spiritually active in the journey. Let's take one more minute to prepare. Take a moment to remember how beautiful the Earth is and how precious life is.

Now imagine yourself leaving the door of your apartment or your house. Start by observing your door turning into a mist, a fog, or even a curtain that you can walk through. It takes you out of your ordinary state of consciousness and leads you into the beauty of the unseen worlds, where the divine beings are waiting to help all of us in this powerful work.

You find yourself walking on a glorious path in nature, where your non-ordinary senses are enlivened and you can see vibrant colors; smell the beauty of the fragrances in nature; see all kinds of magnificent trees, plants, and nature beings; and hear the sounds of nature all around you cheering you on. Even the air tastes so fresh and different than what we experience in our ordinary realm.

As you continue walking, you notice a meadow ahead. You see a big group of people waiting together, welcoming each other, while there are also kind and gentle guardian spirits waiting to greet you.

You notice a giant boat sitting on this meadow. After greeting your fellow companions, the guardian spirits welcome you onto this Spirit Boat, which will be led by divine and loving spirits that will take us all together into the Eye of the Storm.

It is explained to us that we will go through a lot of turbulence, but that this boat is so protected by the helping spirits that everyone is

100 percent safe. So, if you are sensitive at all to turbulence, remember we are being protected, and you are doing this work so you will receive a new tool to help you go through the turbulence that sometimes comes into our lives.

We begin to take off, and we all start singing in the boat. Do you have a favorite song? Singing has been used for thousands of years to bond with others in our community and to bring a sense of grace and joy into any challenge we are facing.

Although you are in a Spirit Boat with others, a helping spirit will be with you to help you in a unique fashion as you journey through the turbulence and together we dive into the storm. We make it into the Eye of the Storm. Just relax and breathe deeply. We made it. You are in the eye. Just feel yourself relaxing into this amazing experience of stillness and peace. You move into such a powerful, calm center that you realize you can attain this state anytime you want. The stillness is holding you, and you feel like you are floating on the softest cloud the sky can offer you.

And now is our time to return. The Spirit Boat turns around, and we fly quickly and with ease over the storm, landing back into the beautiful landscape we started from. You get out of the boat, and with all your companions who were on this journey, you form a circle and hold hands. You look into the light of each other's eyes with gratitude for having a community to share this experience with. And you now know that you can repeat this experience on your own at any time.

Everyone waves goodbye, and you begin your journey back from the meadow, through the aliveness of nature that surrounds you on your path home.

You come to the mist, fog, or curtain and step back through, leaving the non-ordinary realms, back into your home, where you now feel at peace.

Take a moment to think about how you feel, and imagine roots growing out of your feet connecting you with the heartbeat of our four-billion-year-old Earth, who loves you. Feel yourself connected to the sun, the wind, the water, and the moon and stars.

Life on Earth gets turbulent. But there is always a place of peace and rest for us in the Eye of the Storm.

CHAPTER 12
The Blue Hour

Llyn

It's a twenty-minute walk from where I live to the top of a dirt bluff overlooking the Salish Sea. I love gazing out over the water and listening to the waves crash far below. No matter if it's cold or windy, people come here on clear evenings to watch the sunset. Silently, each person looks out to the violet skies and to the fiery sun whose reflection reaches out across the water to us like a pathway home. When the sun disappears, the path of light is gone.

Some of us linger in the chilled air after sundown, immersing in the fleeting magical moments when everything takes on a mysterious blue hue. The world we look out to isn't real anymore; forms seem to shift and morph. The otherworldly atmosphere and the receptive lunar forces invite us to deeply listen and feel. The blue tone communicates a quiet sense of waiting, though for what we do not know.

The larger sphere of night is the heavens. As daylight wanes, we are closer to the celestial. On some nights, we may see countless stars, and on others, no stars are visible. You may remember times in your life that felt void of light, when challenges seemed as dense as a thickly overcast sky. Yet, when all light dims, a limitless part of you still shines, like a star whose light never goes out.

Just as a palpable spirit encompasses the Blue Hour that interfaces day and night, and night and day, a luminous wakeful presence weaves our personal tapestry with life's great mystery. At times when nothing feels stable or right, this Wakeful One knows the dark is brilliant and that we are light.

I encountered my Wakeful One out of the blue as a child. I remember feeling so alone, huddled with my pillow and blanket one night in the small closet my brother and I shared. In my saddest moments, I sensed a presence with me in the darkness.

When our heart is tender, we can close our eyes and take a deep breath. Sensing our Wakeful One with us in the dark, we will feel held by a compassionate universal presence.

The Wakeful One lives at the edges of awareness; it is always close. This quiet one knows all the pathways from dark to light and the many nourishing places to rest. No matter how entangled we may feel or how much we are suffering, our wakeful presence is free. This liberated essence reminds us of the power and love within and all around us every moment, through every circumstance.

The Wakeful One isn't a spirit guide, it's more intimate—one with our own fabric, an awakened aspect of ourselves. A master skin-changer, it travels through all our embodiments and lifetimes. It is eternal, not merely a witness aspect, but illumined conscious intelligence that bridges the finite material world with a greater, deeper, and limitless universal reality.

Like the wakeful quality of twilight, we feel our Wakeful One most vividly in the liminal spaces of this life-dream, in the quiet and in-between moments. We can honor and sense its presence by inviting space into our busy lives. In resting our awareness in our bodies and hearts and relaxing the mind, we cultivate a fertile place of stillness inside, like the potent dusk pause between day and night. In the full, silent spaces, the Wakeful One speaks—not with words but in a warm, relatable language the heart recognizes and trusts.

The Wakeful One guides us through our descent into the rich inner spaces of the soul.

Just as nightfall happens in phases, and the liminal period of twilight is a shifting, morphing time, there are stages to the descent as well as precursors to all Dark Nights of the Soul. In retrospect, the signs are obvious.

As an example, my son, Eben, who is a brilliant artist, was visiting one summer. Inspired by the round, flat stones he found at the beach, Eben painted a human eye on each stone he collected. It was an uncanny feeling seeing the true-to-life eyes staring back at me. Within weeks, almost a decade after an optic nerve crisis that diminished the vision in my right eye, I underwent emergency laser surgery to save the sight in my left eye. Eben later wondered out loud if the eye stones he painted were omens.

Artists are visionaries, sometimes depicting what comes to pass. It's not farfetched to think my son unknowingly tuned into and mirrored through his art what loomed in a field of potentiality unbound by time or space. The language of this field is image, metaphor, symbol, feeling, dreams, and synchronicity.

What is mirrored in the intelligent field can prepare us for descent. As the signals are often beneath our conscious awareness, we may not recognize the subtle reverberations that foretell significant changes in our lives—yet our Wakeful One does.

Although we may feel alone and afraid through our earth walk, our Wakeful One is there to show us the luminous dark wisdom threads, communications from the field. It can guide us through the unlit spaces we must travel to weave a meaningful journey. Our wakeful presence knows the difficult times are pathways to rich interior realms full of light and love just as the nights are lush in natural beauty.

You may want to take a moment to think about signs that foretold an event that really affected you. As you do, let yourself wonder about the messages and gifts they brought.

Having my vision threatened has been humbling and scary. I have compassion for people with vision differences and those who struggle in ways that others can't see. As I believe that my body speaks to me through the language of symptoms and conditions, I had a lot of revelations when I explored the metaphors of my eye crises. I asked myself, "What am I in the dark about?" "What am I stubbornly or innocently blind to, refusing to see?" "What soul callings do I turn a blind eye to because I'm afraid or—because they don't match how I see myself— how others view me?" The challenges, teachings, and gifts of my vision problems are ongoing. They have opened unforeseen opportunities and pushed me to new ways of seeing and being.

The tone of the Blue Hour is melancholic. Just as the descending nighttime brings the loss of daylight and along with it all the connections and activities that happen in the light and warmth of day, our darkest hours are marked by loss. The gifts of our journey are not immediately apparent. It is in the belly of the beast, when we've dropped to the very depths of us, that we may glimpse the spark of our inner light. It is through the Dark Night of the Soul itself that we transform.

The soul doesn't distinguish light from dark or good from bad. Every experience is one to be forged and empowered by. When we are caught in internal or external conflicts that we can't find our way through, it forces to the surface parts of us that may want to fight, hide under the covers, or run. Even when we are completely lost in forgetting, our Wakeful One is there, trying to get our attention, calling to us through the dense layers of who we think ourselves to be. It calls us back, retrieving parts that are lost, angry, or afraid, calling us home, recovering forgotten or suppressed energy and creativity.

Do we not open our eyes to the dark places within, as we fear their brilliance?

Our resistance is porous. It is where our wakeful presence seeps in so we can retrieve from the shadows—bring to the surface—gifts from the underneath world.

Just under conscious awareness, the intelligent field is speaking to us all the time. Some people are naturally attuned to this field. Beyond the personal, they may sense impending collective change. Those who are sensitive straddle the mundane and dreaming worlds. Blue Hour beings may feel the shockwaves of global events before they happen.

Early in 2020, before the pandemic broke out, several people I knew experienced vertigo, grief, and a dread that wasn't linked to anything happening in their lives at the time. They described not being able to sense the future. As my friends shared their experiences, none of us had a clue that our reality was about to fall apart.

Detecting what is to come, even in retrospect, can feel daunting. Yet, it tells us that we are one with the seamless mystery of life. It reminds us of invisible, loving forces here to support us.

The intuitive and seeing abilities, the messages in dreams and the signs in everyday events, are honored by all indigenous cultures. Many have foreseen the great changes we now experience. Like the Blue Hour, this is a liminal shape-shifting time on Planet Earth. Although ominous, it is a magical window beckoning a new way of being.

Night eventually ends. In the wee morning hours, a soft blue light begins to trickle in. Different than the in-between time of dusk that heralds our descent into night, the Blue Hour following darkness prepares us to engage the fiery energy of creation. After the Dark Night of the Soul has incubated and forged us, we must move back into daytime life. Different upon return, we can draw from the shape-shifting forces of the rising sun to re-create ourselves. This inventive time also reminds us that, just as the intelligent field reflects to us the life dreams that are possible, we can propel our dreams into the field. We can imprint upon the unbound realm of potential what we truly desire for us and the Earth. We can change the energy and create a new outcome. The predawn Blue Hour teaches about the power to manifest our dreams and to re-create self and world.

It's most powerful to share our wishes in the language of the field. You can create or imagine or use dream images, symbols, metaphors, and feelings to amplify the field with love, beauty, and harmony. You may want to write, sing, paint, or draw; perform a ceremony, dance, or reflect.

What do you truly wish for on this earth walk?

What would living in a caring human community that honors all life and the Earth feel like?

Send out a clear message in the language of the field. Feel in your heart and body the world you yearn for, as if it already exists.

Also, take actions every day that support your wishes. Bring this reality into being.

Dark forests can appear frightening and dangerous, yet they are also powerful and beautiful. It is said that if you're in the forest long enough, it illumines the darkness that lives inside so you don't project it onto nature anymore. As we come into greater wholeness within, our hearts and bodies entrain with the Earth. We enter the Earth's deep dream of harmony with all life.

Practice

The Blue Hour is a threshold to deeper ways of seeing and being. It opens us to power, beauty, and magic and reminds us that, just as night always follows day, there are endless cycles of light and dark on this human path. This journey-story guides you to feel nurtured no matter how lost you feel. It reveals forgotten pathways of love and power. The more you visit this sacred landscape in your imagination, the more real and accessible it will be.

Imagine wandering in a dense, dark forest. The night air and sounds make you shiver. When you feel most alone, you come upon a luminous spread of mosses. Breathe in the pristine air of this place. Lie upon the spongy moss bed and rest. Sense the loving tree spirits around you. Feel soft moonlight and starlight filter through the trees onto your skin.

Sense the natural harmony and goodness here. Twilight magic suffuses this restorative place.

Take your time. Engage all your senses.

This mossy ground is a haven, a place to rest and be nurtured no matter how lost you feel, no matter what is happening in life.

As you relax on the soft mosses, become aware of your Wakeful One, who is always with you no matter how deep your descent into darkness or forgetting. This wakeful aspect has led you to this sanctuary; it knows countless nourishing spots to rest, places of light and beauty in this mysterious dark forest. Your wakeful presence knows all the pathways between dark and light. It is never lost.

After resting, imagine rising to your feet upon the moss. Feel the spongy wetness. Sense the golden or silvery shimmer of your Wakeful One with you.

Step upon a glowing pathway you somehow hadn't seen before that is well trodden by your Wakeful One. Listen to everything in the forest, and feel the moist earth beneath your bare feet as you move along the path. Smell the aromatic plants that brush your body.

Take your time, feeling every movement your body makes.

Now, begin to sniff a subtle sweetness in the air. The forest opens to a meadow of wildflowers.

Stroll through the meadow of grasses and flowers. A gentle dawn light pervades the sky as the cool night shifts to early morning warmth. Feel protected in this sacred landscape that feels so familiar.

Walk to the edge of the grasslands, through a grove of white birch trees, and into a clearing. Your Wakeful One is with you.

See a small, aged woman sitting on the earth. Next to her is a large clay pot. Behind her stands a humble dwelling. Sweet woodsmoke fills the air.

You recognize this grandmother from another time.

What does the woman look like? What is her clothing? Notice her wrinkled bare feet, hands, and wizened face.

The woman motions for you to sit near her on the earth. What do you feel as you draw close?

If it feels right, gaze into the ancient woman's eyes.

What do you see? What do you feel?

Take a deep breath—all the way into your belly.

This grandmother is the keeper of the power of descent.

The old woman dips her fingers into thick, fragrant mud that sits in the clay pot beside her. She chants in an otherworldly language as she draws a mark on your face. Then another; and more.

The marks awaken the power of the earth within you.

Some strokes also reclaim gifts of rejected parts of you. Others mark wisdom and compassion that have been deepened in you through times of sadness and tragedy.

As the old woman paints your face with the mud, as each line tells its story, feel the strong guiding spirits that are alive in you. As she chants, you hear her speak in your mind.

"You cannot dream yourself or your world back to wholeness without retrieving power from the descent."

Feel your skin tighten as the mud dries on your face. The power of the marks is one with you.

The mud will eventually dry and fall off or be washed away. The energy remains. It may be invisible to others, but you will know the power you carry. Nature and the spirits will know you.

You may want to draw this design painted on your face or create a mask of it in ordinary reality to bring the power of the earth and your strong guiding spirits into everyday life.

The old woman indicates for you to now dig a hole in the earth.

The soil is loose and dark. Feel the earth against your fingers, as musky smells release into the air. As you dig, envision all the good things you want to draw to your life and all the good things you want to see in the world. Feel joy, wakefulness, connection; clearly imagine the beauty of these intentions as if they are real now.

The hole in the earth is a womb to nurture life and where good seeds can be planted.

Open your cupped hands. The grandmother places four kernels of corn into your palms: red, black, yellow, and white.

Close your eyes; feel the energy of the kernels. See their spiritual light. Feel the hopes and dreams for self and world in these kernels. They need to be nourished, just as humanity needs time, love, and understanding to evolve. The old woman shows you how to blow life into the kernels.

Hold the corn to your heart. Take a breath from the very heart of the Earth and feel it course through your heart. Then blow all that life energy from your heart into the kernels. As you do, sense the beauty, joy, harmony, and connection these kernels will germinate.

Tuck the kernels into the soil. Cover them with soil, then pat the earth mound with your hands. Rain and sunlight, the warmth of earth, the air, and the elements will infuse the seeds. The corn will grow, just as the dreams we nurture manifest. Now hold your palms just above your handprints that remain on the soil; feel the energy of your deepest dreams for all life on the Earth stir beneath your palms. Beam from your palms the radiance of care, wakefulness, and harmony. Feel these qualities infuse the seeds and emanate into the future.

Finally, the grandmother asks you to reflect on what you can do in ordinary reality to support these good dreams. What tangible things, large or small, can you do to nourish good dreams for yourself, the Earth, and all life?

Commit to make these happen. Then take some time to thank the grandmother. Feel this ancient one's unconditional love for you. You can visit her at any time. She is in your heart, always with you on your earth walk.

Rise to your feet and stroll back through the birch grove and the tall grasses and flowers in the meadow. Feel the warmth of the morning sun on your head and back. Notice how shiny dewdrops quickly evaporate on the tallest flowers and blades of grass. Sense the silvery or golden glow of your Wakeful One with you.

You are different upon return. You are marked. You are one with the Earth. You have given energy to good dreams for you and all life. You committed to take actions to support these dreams.

Arriving at the edge of the meadow, find the well-worn pathway through the forest, then lie on the warm mosses. Feel the changes in you as you sink deeply into the green moss bed. Feel your Wakeful One, always with you.

This mossy ground is a haven. From this place, you can visit the grandmother at any time. Your wakeful presence knows all the pathways between dark and light, all the magical places to visit and rest and to dream within. You are never lost.

CHAPTER 13
Earth

Sandra

> Human beings are one of the newer species to become
> part of the web of life. Earth herself is 4.6 billion years old.
> And I find it so fascinating that we try to decide what a
> 4.6-billion-year-old living being needs in order to heal.

It is not the Earth that needs healing. As the Earth continues to evolve
as we do, our disconnection from nature is causing climate issues that
would not have occurred naturally. There are so many books and
videos on the power of healing that comes from just lying or walking
barefoot on the earth.

For me, I love to remind people how old Earth is and how we can
simply physically lie on the earth or use our imagination to experience
our heartbeat becoming one with the heartbeat of the Earth. Imagine

what would happen if we all placed our bodies on the earth, becoming one with her heartbeat. And then, of course, we can always place our non-ordinary-reality ears on the Earth and listen to her speak to us.

Walking through the Dark Night of the Soul means doing the inner work we must do to look at the past issues and traumas we are holding on to and also discovering our own eternal beauty and what brought us to this great planet. It is the Earth that sustains us on all levels.

We can approach the Earth and ask, "May I step into your field of energy?" and find ourselves embraced by the love that the Earth has been sustaining us with for all our lives.

When I grew up in Brooklyn, I could not believe how the Earth could be so beautiful. I have this ability—and I thought everyone had it—to see colors in such magnificent frequencies that the beauty of some colors is overwhelming to me. Some colors are so vivid that I start to feel like I am going to faint when I look at them.

Trees growing in Brooklyn brought a brilliance, joy, and presence that made me simply want to sing to them daily. And the birdsongs were simply beyond my imagination. I sang to the sun every morning and the moon every night. I just could not believe the immense beauty I was surrounded by, and I lived in a city!

Once, when I was teaching at a retreat center that I taught at every year in California, there was a staff member who did some of the most accurate and astounding psychic readings I have ever seen. He was definitively tuned in to the frequency of the flow of the universe and could enter this flow to impart amazing information to those seeking guidance.

I was in such a state of turbulence and heartbreak at the time that I made an appointment to work with this psychic. The first thing he said to me was, "Do you remember how you simply could not believe how beautiful the earth was when you were a child? You would dance and sing and be completely overtaken by the beauty of the Earth." He then said to me, "Well, the Earth still remembers your love for her." And this touched me in ways that I can't even explain.

I was a bit new to how nature knows us and speaks to us constantly through omens and signs. I was aware of how the elements gave us the life we needed to thrive. But I was unaware of the consciousness of nature and that it was reaching out to me daily through every word and thought I expressed. I loved to write at this time in my life, and I would write love letters to the Earth, not realizing she was hearing me and that I could communicate with her.

This was to become one of the biggest lessons I have loved learning through the practice of shamanism and teaching the practice to tens of thousands of people around the world. Nature is alive. We are Nature, and beings in nature are talking to other nature beings and partnering with them in touching ways to help one another. For example, a healthy tree will send out a root filled with nourishment for a struggling tree. And ravens and ants have a kind of symbiotic relationship. Fungi play such a healing role for the Earth, and they have such complex forms of communication. And the list of the magic of nature and how it is interconnected and communicating all the time is endless.

As a species that has disconnected from nature, we are lonely and missing so much of the magic that could help us move out of the Darkness of the Soul into a dimension of reality, where nature and humans communicate and partner in a mutually helpful relationship.

Many people today use the term *Gaia* interchangeably for Mother Earth.

Gaia was the Greek goddess of Earth, mother of all life, similar to the Roman Terra Mater (Mother Earth), or the Andean Pachamama, the Hindu Prithvi ("the Vast One"), or the Hopi Kokyangwuti (Spider Grandmother), who—with Sun god Tawa—created Earth and all its creatures.

Gaia is from Ancient Greek, meaning "the Land of Earth." In Greek mythology, Gaia is the personification of the Earth and one of the Greek primordial deities. She is the ancestral mother of all life.

We give so much praise to Gaia, whose name many use today to show their affection for the living being we call Mother Earth. But we don't treat her well. We pour poisons into her. We try to sculpt her instead of allowing ourselves to be sculpted in a way that allows us to blossom into our true beauty.

For many years, I have been teaching and writing my belief that we were born on Planet Earth—Gaia—to be caretakers for her. She teaches us the power of planting seeds and of all the beauty that grows and blossoms from our gardening efforts. For me, this is a literal way to be in service. At the same time, I see the energy we produce from our words, thoughts, and daydreams as seeds we plant into the unseen earthly realm.

As I have shared before, I believe that shamans are gardeners of energy. We create the same beauty in our lives when we learn how to plant the best energetic seeds that will manifest in the life we desire, so that we can truly follow our own soul's journey.

The Earth also offers such important lessons, ones that we rarely understand, about the power of cleansing and the endless cycles of growth and change.

As humans, we feel vulnerable and fear earthquakes, fires, floods, and other climatic events, although they are simply evidence that the

Earth is doing what she needs to do in order to cleanse and plant new seeds. We have so much fear of fire, but fire is how the Earth regenerates.

We wonder what our role is in climate change. And indeed, we have a role, due to our behaviors of polluting the earth, the air, and the water that give us life.

But we also know the Earth has been resculpting herself since the beginning of time. Water now appears where there once was land, and land is taking over bodies of water. Our landscape is constantly changing.

But considering human behavior, will we be able to deal with the issues of drought and floods brought on by the unconscious acts of humans, who are so steeped in ego and greed? There is such a lack of awareness about how we are so simply dependent on the elements.

We need to learn how to act more consciously toward the Earth, and all of life, while at the same time accepting that the body of the Earth is always changing, just like our body does over time. We are all subject to the laws of evolution, and this means change is truly the only constant in our lives here on the Earth.

Know that we can lay our body down upon the earth and be healed by aligning with her frequency. This act is just like placing ourselves in our own river, where we can find our own flow. And life takes on new meaning when we can tune in to how much support we have rather than the universal support we lack.

The beauty of the Earth is in how she destroys what is no longer healthy and what needs to be composted and then protects the land, in its need for rest and restoration, by growing plants no animal or human would dare enter. One example of this is poison oak, which will grow after a fire, thus allowing the earth to rest and not have any life disturbing the ground. When the land is healed, then new life, sometimes never seen there before, starts to grow and is fed by the nurturance of the Earth and all the elements. Part of the teaching of living on the Earth is that death and rebirth and all the phases in between are going on constantly.

The teaching of how the feminine holds both the power of the light and of the shadow is crucial to understanding the cycle of life. Sekhmet is an Egyptian goddess known for her ability to show us the shadow work we must do in our lives. Kali, in the East Indian traditions, is both the creator and the destroyer. Before we can create the new, we must destroy the old. Time is a weaving of creation and destruction.

It is through this state of egoic death that we can experience union with Kali, creating and destroying the entire universe with our breath, sensation, and thought.

And our body is composed of Earth, Water, Air, and Fire. As earth beings, we are a true reflection of the cycles and phases that the Earth is going through. It is always interesting to do a meditation or journey to see how we change with the cycles of the earth where we live.

We can also plant loving seeds in the earth. I like to write the word *LOVE* in the fresh snow covering the ground where I live. I also write it after a big rain. In this way, the energy of love sinks into the earth as a gift of my gratitude for the earth and all it brings. One can bring the gift of flowers and song to honor the Earth, for every living being on this great Earth sings, including Earth herself. We can plant seeds that beautify the places where we live, even if it is simply in a pot of soil in our apartment.

Of course, we cannot forget that Earth, as the feminine, holds both the energy of the loving divine mother and the destructive energy of Kali. It is important for us to bring balance to all areas of life.

When I climbed Mount Shasta and almost got killed by a boulder flying at huge speeds off the top of the mountain, people who were watching shared something interesting about the energy of Mount Shasta.

I had experienced only loving energies while I lived there during my summers, due to my work at San Francisco State University being only a nine-month-a-year job. I stayed with a friend who was a permanent resident and lived in a mountain cabin. I experienced so much love and magic walking through the lush forests. I even visited in winter. During those months, I loved walking in the silence. I could sit on a rock and listen to the bells that the Lemurians would play. The Lemurians are believed to live under the earth in Mount Shasta. They are a race of people similar to the people of Atlantis. Many believe that, although the Lemurian civilization ended, there are Lemurians living in Mount Shasta.

I went on a vision quest in Black Panther Meadows, a popular site for tourists and residents visiting the mountain. One summer, I chose to sit in a small cave carved into the mountain and meditate without food and water for three days. The only energy I experienced was the same peace and silence I experienced walking through the forest during all those earlier years.

But after that climb when I almost lost my life, the other climbers attempting their pilgrimage to the top of the mountain told me that Mount Shasta was known to be loving and healing—below the tree line. People make pilgrimages to Mount Shasta from all over the world for healing. But once you cross the tree line, the energy of Mount Shasta changes, reflecting more of the Kali or Sekhmet energy, which demands us to stand in our true power and face the challenges life brings to all nature beings. The energy can become quite harsh but is still filled with amazing regenerative power of the feminine in all her forms.

Gaia will certainly survive all the coming changes. Civilizations in the past have brought themselves into extinction through their behavior, their actions filled with greed and the desire for control and power.

The Earth has always survived all the changes . . . but will we?

People who live or have lived close to the Earth and receive all their nurturance from the life-forms in their area understand the changing cycles of this planet. They might perform ceremonies for days at certain times of change, like on the solstice or equinox, or during changing phases of the moon. As I have shared, civilizations with this kind of connection to nature were especially astute at watching changing constellations in the sky, which seemingly told them about events that were coming and for which they needed to prepare. Countless ancient and contemporary people, those in sync with the rhythms of the universe, gained knowledge by understanding how the changing stars changed our lives on Earth, too.

We are disconnected from nature, and we give our power to technology rather than learning about nature's flow and timing.

I once brought through a group of spirits called "the Ancient Ones." They are an energy that seems to come through many civilizations. Many of my students have also met them. They are billions of years old, so they hold a completely different perspective on time. They shared with me that our life is less than the blink of an eye to them. They said that the Earth is not aware of the impact we are having on her. Of course, she is changing the climate based on her own needs to cleanse what we are doing, but it's not like she is taking it out on us. She is simply cleansing herself.

I believe as we walk through the Dark Night of the Soul, the simplest of practices are necessary to once again connect with Nature. And showing our love of the Earth is a good way to begin.

Practice

I teach workshops on using spiritual practices to heal the Earth. I wrote about the work in my books *Medicine for the Earth* and *The Book of Ceremony*. Some of my students were inspired from the trainings to make compostable seed pods, where they could place love messages for the Earth in the pods. Some of my students are traveling around the world, planting these seed pods that are typically made from clay.

You don't have to travel all over the world, but you can make a little compostable container for seeds that you blow the energy of love into. Those buried seeds will eventually root in the Earth and grow into beautiful plants filled with the healing power of love.

Another similar practice is finding stones, crystals, gems, and plant spirit offerings that you can sprinkle on places you want to honor. I like to sprinkle blue cornmeal on my walks in beautiful places to give gratitude for my life and to honor the Earth and all the living beings that live in the landscape.

You can blow the energy of love into a rock and leave it by a tree, honoring the earth.

You can blow into little crystals beautiful intentions for all of life and plant these seed crystals in the earth.

A very important practice to incorporate into your life is to either lie on the ground, whether physically or through a meditation or shamanic journey. This is especially effective on the equinox and solstice, because during these times, Earth is experiencing these changing phases exactly as your own body is experiencing them.

Imagining yourself merging with the earth and feeling the change in the quality of her soil, the texture, the smell, the color, the temperature, as well as the feeling of movement or stillness, will help you flow with the changes of seasons. Your body will feel in sync with rather than disconnected from the earth. With each change in seasons, you will experience a time in your life when you must care for what needs to be composted, tended, and planted with the seeds of a new life.

And, of course, you can always simply lie on the earth and align your heartbeat with her frequency. That alone will bring great healing. But if you are interested in learning more and deepening your connection to the Earth, open your invisible senses and ask Gaia for a message about how you can be a caretaker of this planet. Then ask her if she has a personal message for you.

I have some of my students write down the wisdom they learn while performing shamanic journeying and ceremonies. This written record will serve as advice for our descendants, a guide for those in the future on how to get through challenging times.

There have been a variety of ways in which our ancestors shared the wisdom they learned from walking through the Dark Night of the Soul—art, stories, songs, and more. And we can do the same for our descendants. As you try this practice, you might hear the songs of your ancestors letting you know that they have your back. We always have support from Gaia and our ancestors. And we can share our wisdom and plant beauty all over the Earth in return for the gift of our earthly life.

CHAPTER 14

Wild Tortoise

Llyn

One spring day when I was outside playing as a child, I looked up to see a huge turtle slowly ambling out of our neighbor's field. I loved the small woodland turtles I found in muddy creeks, but I had never seen such a large turtle. It looked like a miniature dinosaur under thick oval armor. I called for my dad, who ran out the door and down the porch steps to sit with me on the grass to watch it. He said not to get near the snapper as it could bite off our fingers.

Turtles live by water. The snapping turtle had walked miles from its river home to bury its eggs in a sandy mound amid the tall grasses I ran through with my childhood friends.

In the United States, we call turtles that live only on the land *tortoises*. Turtles and tortoises are reptiles and can't adjust their body heat. They need to be in the sun to warm up and in the shade to cool down. Our own body temperature maintains homeostasis by adjusting itself depending upon our environment, yet our feelings aren't always in equilibrium. Tortoises will get sick and die if they can't balance their internal temperature. The level of harmony we feel inside is just as important.

For two months last year, I struggled through a debilitating reaction to a vaccine. I felt like I was moving through an initiatory gauntlet, unsure of whether the continuous pain, exhaustion, and scary neurological symptoms would ever end. I was relieved to finally recover. Just as I felt better, a family member was diagnosed with a life-threatening cancer. Within weeks of this, my young adult nephew who was full of life and promise died without warning of a congenital condition.

These events occurred against the backdrop of social and global chaos, including a pandemic.

I'm not the only one who's felt utterly overwhelmed in facing personal misfortunes and heartbreaks while also dealing with the rapid changes in our societies and on the planet.

Wild Tortoise came to me in a dream when life felt so fragile and as I was healing and grieving at the same time.

I stand in the center of a large circle of sand, marked on four sides by the directions. An expansive forest lies beyond the circle. I look down to see a tiny tortoise on the sand at my feet. I pick up Tortoise and stand holding it through many decades as it grows. I eventually bend forward and release the now-very-large being back to the earth. I watch as Tortoise slowly ambles across the sand into the trees.

Turtles and tortoises can live more than two centuries. They are the oldest living beings on our planet, and their species dates back millions of years. Imagine that you hold a tiny tortoise in your arms. Feel as if you can merge with its ancient wisdom as you safeguard it through the decades it takes for a wild tortoise to mature—just as people need time and support for their wisdom to grow.

We live at an amazing and evolving time on Planet Earth. I've witnessed this in my own life: aspects of myself that need changing often get worse or come into crisis before they get better. During these times, I can also be pushed in directions I hadn't considered or was resistant to, yet which have helped me live in more healthy and authentic ways. Such transitions can cause me a lot of stress. Even good changes can bring discomfort and loss. These are times of great promise, yet we are in the peak of the turbulent phase of change when our reality can feel turned upside down, like a tortoise lying on its back. There is a saying that a tortoise lying upside down can't get up. This isn't true. The tortoise uses its strong neck muscles to right itself. Tortoise medicine can help us find stability when life feels overturned, as our reality reconstructs itself.

A wild tortoise will pull its limbs and neck into its shell for protection. Yet, its hallmark is the vast distance it can wander in an unhurried pace. Turtle and Tortoise are prime symbols for the Earth. On four sturdy feet and legs that traverse the land, Wild Tortoise embodies the stabilizing power of the earth.

Tortoise medicine helps us stay grounded through the personal and collective transitions we all face now. As we step through chaos, loss, and confusion, we can wander like Tortoise in a timeless practice that synchronizes mind and body and opens us to the Earth's healing forces.

In traditional spiritual wanderings, walkabouts, and pilgrimages, people embark upon a spiritual rite of passage. The journey begins by leaving the familiar behind. In walkabouts, one enters the uncharted territories of the land and unfamiliar regions of heart and spirit. On pilgrimage, one often follows the well-trodden pathways of sages and saints. Walking in their footsteps, we are steeped in a living field of intention and prayer that activates internal mystical terrains. Both walking journeys help us embrace deeper rhythms of life and nature. They stir spiritual aspects of us that may be asleep.

Like Tortoise—and the pilgrims of all times and cultures—in moving slowly across the land, we harmonize with nature. As the subtle pathways between us and the earth open, an inner mandala is illuminated. We can follow this spiritual inner pathway, organizing our thoughts and feelings around its light. Through our movement and by gaining a calmer inner state, the archetypal power of our journey comes alive to guide us.

We may live in a natural setting, yet walking in a park or even down our street is helpful. When we're struggling, it can feel nearly impossible to walk; our legs may feel weak in carrying our heavy and despairing heart. So, we walk at a tortoise's pace.

We can step over a threshold stick to acknowledge our walk as a pilgrimage. We can recite a simple prayer as we walk. Then, we feel every movement of our body as we step deliberately and open our heart and senses to everything around us. We imagine feeling beneath our feet into the very heart of the Earth.

Over time, a palpable sense of the Earth's heart will come alive for us. We may feel each footstep as if it were a prayer, a gentle thump against the giant healing drum of our Earth Mother. The rhythms reverberate through our body. We may sense life's eternal and cosmic rhythms. We can open to feel held by these ancient pulses, knowing the heart of the heavens is also one with us.

Walking in nature to connect with its balancing forces is healing. It is a simple way to feel held as we move through pain, loss, and disorientation. We are enfolded by ancient alchemical arms that guide us as we walk through dismemberment to a greater wholeness and light.

In placing one foot after the other, we become more embodied. The soft knowing of our inner mandala, the lighted pathway or labyrinth within us, will grow.

We may still feel tender. Yet the dense, heavy suffering will be a little more spacious.

We may still feel uncertain. Yet our breath will be fuller, and our presence will grow through the slow merging with our Earth Mother.

How do we move forward from here? As we feel more connected with the Earth and everything around us, strength seeps into our aching heart.

If we cannot go outside and walk, we can close our eyes and imagine walking to greet the trees and plants in our neighborhood. Or we can pick up a drum and softly beat with our fingers and palms the rhythms of our walk, feeling these reverberate through our body. Over time, we become one with this rhythm, and our mind and heart entrain with the mandala, the lighted pathways within us.

You may draw or paint or create a collage of the beautiful inner mandala that you see, sense, or intuit. When feeling confused or lost, gaze at the image or trace its pattern with your fingers until your feelings and whole being come into coherence with the design.

Wild Tortoise is a seed bearer. It plants beautiful trees, ground cover, and essential fungi. It is also an amazing land engineer; through its burrowing, it creates homes for countless species. This placid, solitary creature infuses our world with life, organization, and beauty.

Like Tortoise, we can spread good seeds. We can keep beauty alive in our heart and vision amidst the pain in our lives and through whatever plays out all around us.

Wild Tortoise is a living representation of the sacred circle and the four sacred directions of the Earth—under the circle of its shell are its four strong legs. It is thought that Tortoise, with its sensitive feet, may even detect low vibrational sound waves that travel through the Earth.

Another way Tortoise guides us to find our balance with nature as we navigate change and challenge is by centering us within the sacred circle and four directions. If we live near land where we can wander, find a place that calls to us, make offerings, and ask permission to sit at this spot. With a stick or by sprinkling cornmeal, draw a circle on the ground. Invoke and mark the four directions with small stones, and sit in the circle's center. Then rattle, drum, or sing, or be silent and still. Over time, we will feel that we are in a relationship with everything around us. We may receive a message from the earth as the subtle pathways between us open.

Early in 2011, I was told that I needed to have portion of my skull removed then reattached as part of a major surgery to take out a tumor pressing against the optic nerve of my right eye. After the surgery, I would undergo cancer treatment, as the mass was likely malignant. My recovery would take a year. Upon receiving this news, I became literally sick with dread.

I went to the forest to find my center. The wind rustled through the tree branches as rain softly fell. Leaves glistened all around, and the air smelled fresh and musky. I placed a threshold stick on the ground and stepped over it into the forest. My heart felt as raw as the weather. I wandered for a time, then ventured off the path, until I found the place that called. I made offerings to this place and asked if I could sit for a while. I drew a sacred circle and invoked the directions. Then I sat on the earth in the center of the circle and cried. The rain cried with me. My face was dripping wet. I tasted on my lips the salty tears mixed with pure, sweet rainwater.

My breath, thoughts, and shaking body finally settled.

I begged the earth and trees to help me find peace and courage.

I sat in stillness, listening with my whole heart and body.

Through a prolonged period of quietness, I began to feel the earth. I sensed she also felt me. I let go even more, as if I could lean back into the comfort of my Earth Mother's arms. My breath deepened and a sense of well-being came over me.

Over time, a knowing seeped in. The trees and the earth were telling me something. A gentle energy pulsated through me and slowly formed into words:

"My body does not have the vibration of cancer."

After hearing them in my mind, I spoke the words out loud.

"My body does not have the vibration of cancer."

I sensed the rightness of this in my being, an unshakable trust of what nature was telling me.

The next week, upon seeing a different specialist, I was told, "This isn't cancer. Furthermore, it's inoperable because of its location."

I dedicated the next nine months to shamanic practice and ceremony, holistic therapies, dream reflection, and nature-based work. Within this time, I also found a minimally invasive treatment to shrink my benign tumor.

As we draw sacred circles for ourselves, we can also draw them for someone else who is suffering. We can place a piece of paper with the person's name on it in the center of a circle drawn with flower petals, cornmeal, or small stones. It can sit on your altar, in another dedicated place in your home, or on land. You may drum, rattle, perform ceremony over the circle, or simply ask an ally to help.

When my children were in their twenties, I placed pieces of paper with their names written on them under a palm-size rattle on my altar. A dolphin shape is carved on top of the ceramic piece. I lit a beeswax candle, held my hand over the turquoise dome, and asked Dolphin to guide and protect my children. I did not tell anyone this. The next day, in speaking with my daughter, she told me about her dream of that night. In the dream, she was swimming across a huge expanse of water. The task was hard, yet Sayre was happy because swimming right beside her was a dolphin who had come to guide and protect her.

Our prayers, wishes, and intentions carry energy. The spiritual beings and protective circles we invoke are real; they impact the subtle and the material worlds.

Now, many years later, the dolphin rattle still sits on my altar with my children's names tucked beneath it.

Be sure to include the names of nature beings, social situations, and aspects of life needing prayers. A ceramic or wooden bowl can sit inside the circle so the "prayer slips" can rest in the bowl. Alternatively, you can place prayer slips in a pouch or satchel that rests within the circle. Our healing community has witnessed profound miracles through this lovely ritual that is so easy to do. It's important to also extend our blessings beyond people to nature and all sentient life.

The unhurried, solitary Tortoise has been a steady guide to help me come back to my sacred center and to the Earth. Tortoise medicine is an embodied path. Inseparable from body are the profound mystical aspects of who we humans really are, reminding us that we are one with Spirit and that we must eventually transcend physical life.

Tortoise's cosmic shell design, with its thirteen segments, is seen by some cultures as related to the thirteen moons cycle and likewise is said to depict a map of the afterlife.

Wild Tortoise follows the Earth's magnetic fields back to its original home. Our walkabouts connect us with the Earth's magnetism and open ancient inner pathways that take us home to ourselves. Wild Tortoise must adjust its course as the Earth's magnetic fields are shifting. As our world shifts and changes, its spirit can help us find our way.

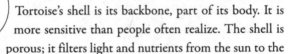

Practice

Tortoise's shell is its backbone, part of its body. It is more sensitive than people often realize. The shell is porous; it filters light and nutrients from the sun to the body and its organs. Through its earth walk, the Tortoise absorbs telluric forces: it receives cosmic energy through its shell.

The shell of our human body is also sensitive and porous. Through our skin, movement, and our breath, we absorb vital life energies from the Earth and heavens.

On a sacred journey I facilitated many years ago, renowned Maya elder Tata Pedro Cruz Garcia taught us to honor the Earth, heavens, and the elements as we also draw in and activate their restorative forces within us. Here's a practice Tata shared to embody this wisdom:

> Stand tall and take a deep breath in and out. Gently bend forward, extending your arms and hands to the ground as if you can touch deeply into the earth. Breathe in deeply, then say:
> "Oh, Heart of the Earth!"

Slowly straighten your body and reach with your hands and arms above you, imagining you touch the heavens. Breathe in, then say:

"Oh, Heart of the Heavens!"

Slowly bring arms and hands down to extend them to your left side as you also slightly turn your torso to the left. Motion with your hands as if you are collecting life force from the water. Breathe in, then say:

"Oh, Heart of the Sacred Waters!"

Slowly bring arms and hands back to you, then extend them out to your right side as you turn slightly to the right. Motion with your hands as if you are collecting life force from the fire. Breathe in, then say:

"Oh, Heart of the Sacred Fire!"

Slowly face forward again and bring both hands to your heart. Then open, arms outstretched to either side of your body. Rotate them in circles as if absorbing with your hands the sacred winds blowing through them. Breathe life force into your own wind chambers, your lungs, then say:

"Oh, Heart of the Sacred Winds and the Four Directions!"

Draw your hands in and rest your palms over your heart. Take a deeply centering breath. Say:

"Our Hearts!"

To close, make a simple bow to acknowledge the living forces within and all around you.

Doing this practice outside with bare feet is ideal. It's also fine to be inside. Be sure to move slowly, like a tortoise. Breathe deeply, and feel nature's energy come alive in you with every breath in and out. Feel oneness expand throughout your being.

If you must sit, just move as you are able. You can also simply imagine and feel the practice if you can't move or need to lie down. Open your heart to the vital forces all around and within you.

Our bodies are made of the earth and the elements, and we are one with even the most distant star. Through our practices, we can awaken and embody the cosmic as well as terrestrial qualities that lie dormant within us—for strength and balance, and to take our respectful place in the sacred circle of life.

Half of all wild turtle and tortoise species are threatened with extinction. The largest threats are the loss of habitat and climate change.

How do we move forward from here? We can make our earth walk conscious and honor the amazing beings we share this planet with. We can help others working to protect and cultivate biodiverse lands so wild tortoises and other nature beings will thrive.

As we preserve our threatened wildlife, we also nourish the vulnerable and endangered aspects of humanity.

CHAPTER 15
Rose

Sandra

> I have always had this fascination—or should I say love—
> for roses.

My father had an extraordinary green thumb. One would not expect that a Brooklyn typewriter repairman would have so much magic in his hands. He could grow such amazing flowers and magnificent vegetables, so beautiful that they looked too perfect to be real.

It was his love to come home from work and get his hands deep into the earth. The soil taught me so much about the power of love we emanate as opposed to the power of love we say through words. My father had a very traumatic life and was not the best at verbal communication. But the amazing garden my father created and his remarkable paintings showed me his love for beauty and life. This energy emanated in such a way as to show me that healing can be born through the creations we make with love. Words are not always necessary.

When I was in junior high school, we were reading *Le Petit Prince* by Antoine de Saint-Exupéry. I fell in love with this little book, filled with so much wisdom. I memorized the book in both French and English, and I still continue to read it today. For me, as for so many others, one part of the book captured my heart. In the story, there is a teaching that the rose gives the Little Prince: "It is only with the heart that one can see rightly; what is essential is invisible to the eyes."

Between my father's gift for growing roses and the heartwarming quote from *The Little Prince*, I have always been in awe of roses. I love their fragrance and recently have learned that our brains also love their fragrance. Apparently, our brain physically responds to the smell of a rose. And, of course, we can think of Rose as a great teacher of boundaries, given its thorns. Rose tells us that we must tread carefully in the energy field of others unless we have permission. The thorns of a rose keep out those she does not want in her sacred space. When we see the colors of roses and are allowed to touch their silken leaves, they inspire within us all kinds of emotion. Roses are associated with romance, love, beauty, and joy.

Rose took me in her loving embrace as I was walking on my journey through the Dark Night of the Soul. Due to the condition that I have, I can't lay my head down to rest. So, rest is a huge issue. There are days when this isn't a problem for me. But I have had days when not being able to rest my head or feel rest in my body felt like real torture—and it is real torture.

On one of my journeys, a bright red Rose reached out to me as I was walking through the darkness. I did not feel the Rose literally reach out to touch me, but I felt her energy field embracing me. And she told me that smelling the fragrance of a rose would bring me the rest that I needed. As a healing tool, it sounded a bit unrealistic to me, but due to my love of roses, I tried it. When I took in the deep rose fragrance, I felt my body relaxing, just as Rose promised.

All plants are great teachers of accepting life, death, and impermanence. Their lives are typically short, so we can watch their entire cycle—beginning from planting the seed, through germination and watching the first sign of life emerge from the deep earth, to blossoming into its true glory, to ending up as compost, to feeding the earth again so new life can be born.

Everything on this planet is always changing. The sun rises and sets each day, the wind currents change, the ocean tides ebb and flow, the Earth is always creating and destroying life-forms. The moon moves into her fullness and then retreats into darkness. Then there is the beautiful sliver of the new moon. The seasons change. Our vegetation changes. Migration of different birds and animals come and go. Storms come and go, changing the landscape of nature constantly over time. Then we have dusk, which is so powerful because it is that magic time myths have been written about. It is an in-between time where mystery lives.

Nature teaches us that life is in constant change, and that is just life. Nature flows with the changes rather than resists. What is no longer healthy is removed from this earth, and then the earth re-creates new life forms as others die out.

Nature has its flow, and finding our own flow is essential to our health and well-being. We often put ourselves into the river of the collective instead of finding our place in our own river. As we explore pace and flow, we learn even more about life's changes.

In our modern Western culture, most people no longer know the language of nature, as people who lived so close to the land once did. We watch nature from afar, take photos when we see something of beauty, hug or sit by a tree. But rarely do we drop into the same type of communication that all nature beings have with each other. Through invisible communication and a greater connection to the web of life, nature beings partner with each other in different ways and help each other survive.

As I wrote earlier, trees, plants, insects, and fungi share restorative nurturance. Many insects and plants have such symbiotic relationships. For example, colorful plants and bees, butterflies, beetles, and ants are much more complex than we realize. And the list goes on. But we tend to be very lonely creatures, isolated from the rest of nature. We feel that we are watching nature, as if we are separate. Due to our lack of connection, some people take this to an extreme degree, believing that humans are the most evolved species and have the power of life and death over other life forms on Earth. The fact is that this planet is an intricate and magnificent weaving-together of all of life. When we perceive ourselves as separate, we may miss some of the greatest lessons about creation, dissolution, impermanence, and death.

Everything in existence flows and changes, which means that everything, every state we experience in life, isn't permanent. There's always birth, dissolution, and death. We experience a constant flow of change on Earth. We can learn so much by accepting this state. Then, as we enter and begin to flow in harmony with ourselves and the river of life, we can reflect on what we are resisting. This is a big key—we must learn how to flow rather than resisting the changes that life brings us. Once you have found your flow, if you find yourself entering a change you don't like or that doesn't serve you, you can make a new choice to move into a healthier path.

But if you resist, you get stuck. As a result, you end up creating more pain by keeping yourself rigid. Pain reflects stuck energy. Once we move into a flow, we can then flow with the changes. In this state, we don't hold ourselves back or get twisted up by trying to resist the constant change.

Part of entering back into life after resisting is learning how to flow with and grow through changes in a graceful way. This includes learning that even when you are in the flow, life might bring you situations and events that you can't change but must learn to accept. Accepting what life brings for us means understanding that everything in life is impermanent. When change comes, we must remember that we don't understand the big picture or what the gift of change will ultimately bring for our own growth and evolution. The change we might want to resist may bring us wisdom about how to live a more authentic way of life.

I watch so many people get to a comfortable place in life, and they believe that their good fortune will be permanent. But when we connect with nature fully, we learn that to hold on to only what is good, thinking it will never change, is pure illusion.

There is always a place to stop and try to fight, to explore all possible solutions to the darkness in our life. But again, sometimes in the impermanence of life, we must learn to accept both what brings us joy and what brings us to deep suffering. If we hold out for permanent states of bliss, we most likely will be disappointed, because everything in life changes constantly.

The changes we experience in life keep moving us forward toward our death. As nothing is permanent here on Earth, neither is our life. And as I have been sharing, when we go through any kind of initiation, especially one that has you walking through the darkness, you continue to die to yourself. As the great universal plan works with the blueprint of our destiny, life brings us so many situations that simply wear us down. There is no way out when we think of practical solutions, and there is no way out if we just try to power through. We can feel quite trapped and hopeless.

But this is where the powers of impermanence and acceptance can be our allies. When we go through trials, we end up dying to some part of ourselves, and that not only carves us into a new person with greater resilience and capacity for change but also one who understands that death on all levels is simply another rite of passage.

When I was on my longest walk through the darkness, I was told by my helping spirits that, in the end, I would either be dust or a polished stone. And I think that is true for all of us. Our journey through life leads us through so many paths—paths lined with the energies of bliss, suffering, and disappointment. As we walk through the dark places in our life and accept our losses, we die to what the ego and mind mistakenly think is the best life path for us. The darkness helps us touch into our vulnerabilities, and each loss allows us to die just a little more, so that when life takes from us, creation brings something new into our lives. Any life form that stops growing dies.

In nature, death is not an end. Death only leads to new creation, opening doors to new dimensions of reality. This is true whether we physically leave our bodies to engage in a new adventure of life or if we stay here as a polished stone ready to be kind to ourselves and be in service to all of life.

Practice

Following the Life of a Seed

It is a fascinating process to experience the entire life cycle of a plant. It offers us a view into our own cycle of growth. You can pick your favorite plant to journey to in a beautiful place in nature. Play some spiritual music or allow the silence to carry you into a state of deep contemplation. This meditation has an organic flow, so don't get caught up in following directions. Go with the grace-ful dance of creation, and see what happens.

A seed of beauty of a healing plant is placed into the ground by the wind or by an insect that drops it on its journey. The seed is nurtured by the earth and eventually moves into a process of germination. It experi-ences its first initiation as it struggles to pop up through the dark, thick soil. As it is fed by the sun, wind, rain, moon, and love of creation, it has an easy time growing. In its desire to live, it continues to grow and withstand the challenges of the elements. It grows deep roots into the earth, strength-ening the connection to the earth that gives it so much life. The plant moves into a season of blooming, where it finally faces the sun in deep gratitude for its life here. And as the plant ages and the elements begin to wear it down, it eventually leaves its body behind and returns to spirit.

Part of walking through the darkness means needing to learn self-care. There is the struggle of the new birth of consciousness, but we have the sun to feed us with light to grow, blossom, and heal. The water and wind bring us life and strengthen us and the earth helps us root fully into life. The moon also impacts our ability to heal.

One thing about nature, and this includes us, is that we were born with the DNA blueprint of how to have a healthy body. All of nature is born with this blueprint. I have watched crystals that were cracked heal over time. And although not all illness is curable, a lot of our current issues could be solved by getting into the flow of nature.

A plant needs rest and sun, and so do we. After a long walk through the Dark Night of the Soul, it is good to remember that you are like a plant and that you need rest and sun. Maybe you can find a beautiful Rose who wishes to help you rest.

If you would like to perform this journey again, put on some sha-manic music, and make a choice whether you would like to dance or sing or sit or lie down passively during this experience. You are going to set your intention to merge with a seed and to learn about the life of a seed by becoming the seed. You germinate and begin to move up through the earth, and you feel the power of the sun and moon. What supports your growth? What takes away from it?

How does the rain, the mist, the fog affect you? How does the wind feel on your leaves? Follow the plant through its entire life process, from the moment the seed was placed into the ground until its eventual death and return to the earth. This is a powerful journey to learn about birth, growth, impedance, and death.

One purpose of this journey is to give a sense of nature's life cycles. But I am also suggesting it so that you can reflect on being a plant at this time on the planet. What do you need for your regeneration while walking through the Dark Night of the Soul? I wonder what ally or allies will show up for you.

And I wonder how the allies you meet along your walk through the Dark Night of the Soul will help prepare you for when you will leave the planet.

Life is filled with initiations that lead to death while we are alive or physical death, where we leave this world and return to Source and are welcomed home again.

Journey to the Sea to Learn about Impermanence

Water teaches us to understand impermanence. In spiritual traditions where this is an essential teaching, the ocean is often used as a teacher.

In this journey, we are going to work as we have in previous chapters. In Chapter 11, we met on a meadow where a Spirit Boat awaited us, ready to take us to the primal sea together. Once we have been through darkness, we need a community to welcome us back into engaging in life as a changed person. We have returned with new morals, ethics, ways we wish to live our life, and passions. It doesn't matter when you are reading this book, because as I have mentioned before, we are working outside of time and space. Whenever you participate, our ceremony is still going on.

Use your shamanic instrument or listen to some music, sing or dance, or remain passive. Imagine leaving your apartment or house through your door, which shape-shifts into a mist, fog, curtain, or veil. It brings you from the ordinary realms into the magic of the timeless transcendent realms. You walk up the path to a meadow. You have been there before, to this place covered with beautiful wildflowers, with the wind blowing and the sun shining brightly on you.

You meet all of us at the meadow. There are guardian spirits waiting to greet us and inviting us onto the boat. This is no ordinary boat; it is a Spirit Boat made of wood and decorated with symbols of power, strength, and love. We will be guided to the primal sea that gave everything life on this Earth. Notice how the boat feels to you—the mystery, the power, the strength, the magic. We gaze at the sea, in awe of her beauty.

We leave the boat and ask the water if we can step into her field of energy, light, and beauty. And when the boat lands, we run to put our hands in these ancient loving waters. We wash our face in them. And we feel we are home.

As you continue to play with the water and pour it over your head, continue to make a connection with her. Tell her how you feel about her.

As children, we used to love to play in the sand, and if you remember doing this, join in with all of us as we draw symbols of love that the primal sea will take and share with all the waters of the world. This love will go to every creature, every coral reef, invertebrate, algae, plankton, fish, shark, whale, dolphin, and the many beings that live in the sea that we don't even know about it. It's amazing to hear mysterious creatures that have adapted to living in depths that we can't even imagine. Draw symbols of honor, beauty, respect, care, commitment.

The waters of the seas will eventually work with other forces in nature to bring moisture to all land creatures, such as my ally the Rose, who always holds space with unconditional love for me no matter what I am going through.

The cycles of life are continuous, and the magical alchemy of how each being on Earth is nurtured and cared for is nothing less than extraordinary.

Now, stand back as the mighty sea comes. First, she sprays water on you with love and support. Laugh with her. Then she laps over all your exquisite, stunning, lovely symbols, all the way deep, deep, deep down to the unseen currents, as we together hold hands and welcome each other back into the light after such a long journey through the darkness.

Before we leave, ask the primal sea, "Do you have a message for me about birth, death, and impermanence? Do you have advice for me about living in turbulent times? Do you have any guidance about learning how to walk through the darkness while riding the waves of change?"

It is now time to leave. We smile at each other as we get back on our Spirit Boat carrying us gracefully back to the meadow. We all leave the boat and say goodbye. You might notice that you no longer feel so alone as you enter your home.

CHAPTER 16
Nootka Lupine

Llyn

Springtime in the Hoh River valley is magical. The earth has softened after the long, cold winter, the river runs wildly, and streams and waterfalls are swollen. In heading down the footpath from the cabin, salmonberry blossoms, velvety thimbleberry leaves, and the supple new growth tips of evergreen branches tickle my skin. The trees abruptly end as the trail opens to a sandy dale that was once the river floor. Plush banks of glacial silt stretch across the lands to foothills draped in mist. Stones coated in powdery silt lie everywhere. Beyond silt beds and rock gullies, the main river channel rages.

Only hardy plants can tolerate the coarse earth and harsh winters of the Hoh gravel bar. Each year, more willow trees show up in this part of the valley. Their tenacious roots can grip through packed layers of stone, and the slender, bendy branches of the willow won't break in the wind.

Resilient and delicate, as well, is one of my favorite plants, the Nootka lupine. I scan the ground each spring to find the merry stalks studded with blue-violet pea-shaped flowers. At the base is a chaotic splash of greenery. Sparkling water beads cling to lupine's furry tapered leaflets that fan out in five to eight pointed stars. My heart gushes.

The Nootka lupine is a tender contrast to the unproductive soils and weather extremes where it grows. Its deep taproot allows it to drink water and nutrients from fertile, hidden pockets in the earth.

At times of uncertainty, when you feel like you're holding on for dear life, imagine the lupine's steadfast taproot. Nothing that plays out on the surface can touch this lush underneath space. Imagine smelling the rich earthen scents. Open your heart to this protected, abundant pocket. Breathe in nature's nourishing force. Trust that you will have what you need and feel protected through this time.

Even though it lives in poor soil, Nootka lupine produces nutrient-dense, beanlike seeds that are healthy to eat after they are boiled and soaked.

Lupine teaches about being wealthy inside, giving out beauty and richness no matter the situation. Tulalip Native American oral historian and master storyteller Johnny Moses speaks to this in tales about his great auntie, a Nuu-chah-nulth (Nootka) tribal member who lived on Meares Island in British Columbia.

"There is an elderly lady whose name was Philomena Jackson. Philomena Jackson was a blind lady. Yet, she could weave beautiful baskets. She could feel the colors as she was weaving. She'd be weaving, and she would sing beautiful songs. And she would look out the window, the east window. She was always looking out the window as she was weaving her baskets. She lived all by herself in this house. She would get a strong feeling and start to fix her fire, tend to her fire so it would be just right. And she would cook clam chowder, salmon, whatever. . . .

"She knew her house so well. She lived in that house for many years; thirty-three years she lived in this house. She felt her house with her hands. When she first moved in, she felt everything in her house, even the ceiling and even the floor. She got on her hands and knees to feel the feelings of the wood in the floor. She said it took her one year to study her house, to make friends with her house. Now she knows where everything is. She would move around in her house just like she could see. She would start cooking. She never burned herself. That was amazing."

Like Nootka Lupine, no matter our limitations, we can root into a wealth of goodness.

Like Philomena Jackson, we can open the eyes of our heart and be in intimate relationship with the ordinary details of our lives.

We can appreciate every part of our home. Even if it is a humble home, we are blessed. Many people don't have homes. We may be inspired to live more simply. We may find joy in preparing home-cooked foods. Making friends with our home slows us down. When more present and fulfilled, we look outside of ourselves less and have more to give. We may feel compassion for neighbors and friends who are struggling. Do they need anything? Have they slept and eaten? Do they have someone to be with and talk to?

Tending to the everyday and creating a relationship with our environment is sacred work. It connects us with the gifts that are right here with us. As we look through the eyes of the heart, we see that abundance and goodness are always there. Like Auntie Philomena, this propels us to sing and weave even more beauty back into the world.

There is richness to be tapped in every moment and especially when we most need it, in the wintry phases of life.

During Johnny's stays with her, his auntie Philomena told him, "The winter is very important. Look at the food we store away, the food we dry, the dried salmon, dried meat, dried berries. But once we put the food in water, once we cook the food, it is rich again. Winter is to remind us we can be rich again. Our spirit can be full of riches. . . .

"This time [winter] reminds us every year of how rich we really are. How much is stored away for us like our food, our dried food that we store away to prepare for the winter. We have a lot of gifts stored away that we do not know about. Somewhere, sometime, your ancestors put away some knowledge for you to use, to eat on, to live on."

Winter teaches us to find light in the dark, spiritual resources that are here to nourish and guide us.

I've had several wintry seasons in life including throughout childhood. One five-year period as an adult was particularly challenging, ultimately pushing me to leave the life I knew behind to live in the Hoh rain forest. Before this, with all the major life transitions and losses I experienced, I kept thinking about getting a tattoo. Although I had never wanted a tattoo, I felt that a symbol could mark this passage with power and give me courage. I wondered what image to choose.

During this time, I presented at a program in Vancouver, Canada. In a dream the first night, I had a clear vision of characters drawn in black ink. I knew this was the symbol I was looking for. The following morning, before the conference, I brought my room key to the front desk of the university housing. The day was warm, and the welcomer wore a sleeveless top. On her left upper arm was the symbol. I told the young student I had just seen the image in a dream, and I asked if she would mind sharing with me the meaning of her tattoo. She graciously told me that she had it done during a very tough time in her life. The Japanese kanji writing translated as "perseverance" gave her the strength to keep going.

I've heard many such tales over the years. Auspicious direction can appear when we most need it and connect us with the underlying power of our journey.

Enduring Nootka Lupine helps us hold strong. Its resilient spirit tells us that we can always tap into a wealth of goodness.

As another example, in 2001, my children and I were heartbroken to leave our friends and family as well as the beautiful mountain we lived on to move to another state for their dad's work. My son, who was ten at the time, kept saying he needed a sword. Not a play sword but a real one. Eben wanted a sword so intently that his sister, Sayre, drew a beautiful picture of a sword for her brother to dream with. Some months later, Eben saw something glint in the pond behind our house. Under the water on the sandy bottom lay a sword. Eben didn't get to keep the authentic relic, as it was placed in a museum. Yet its energy and power were clearly with him.

Compassionate helping spirits and energies may come to us in dreams in the form of symbols or icons, or they may show up tangibly. The material and spiritual worlds are not separate.

Auntie Philomena reminds us of the many gifts stored away for us in preparation for leaner times. The knowledge of the ancestors is passed through story and teachings, auspiciously or even through esoteric ways. In many traditions, spiritual gifts were placed in stones, within the earth, in water and trees, and even in the air and space for times of need. Wise grandmothers and grandfathers of the distant past held great empathy and understanding. They stored away like dried food what would spiritually nourish and strengthen people in future times.

The lupine plant is a reminder of these gifts stored in the earth and by the ancestors—and the gifts that lay hidden within us that we can use, eat, and live on through wintry times in life.

Johnny Moses, whose traditional name is *Whis.stem.men.knee* (Walking Medicine Robe), was raised in a remote Nuu-chah-nulth village on the west coast of Vancouver Island, British Columbia, Canada. Auntie Philomena has told Johnny of the grandmothers "who cry so hard, then they laugh so hard. They want to enjoy the riches fully. They want to practice the medicine fully. They want to enjoy every minute, every day, every year they are on this earth."

There's enough heart wisdom in this one quote to feed me for a lifetime. I know the full, rich feeling inside of crying so hard then laughing so hard. Then there are times when the tears just won't flow, and I forget how to laugh. It's good medicine to fully enjoy the riches of every moment here on Earth.

Nootka Lupine encourages us to find the fullness of who we are and to nurture a soulful life. It reminds us to thrive through whatever our journey brings. A phytoremediation plant, lupine enriches the sandy soil and purifies toxins in the land through its own body. Just like the cleansed, fertile soil that lupine creates, the inner wealth we cultivate radiates out.

Nootka lupine, a dainty plant growing in isolated clumps, is part of the restoration process of the land. The limitations of an infertile environment do not deter lupine. It still creates beauty.

The many plants on the Hoh gravel bar that work together with lupine, like willow and others, hold and enliven the soil. They create a fertile foundation for other plants to grow. Similarly, it can give us strength to remember that it has an impact when many of us work together over time. We may feel lost in our own problems or wonder why we were born during such an unstable time on the planet. Yet, there is so much richness here to support us, and we each have, stored away inside, amazing gifts to help monumental change.

Concrete examples of how we can honor these gifts and the beautiful lupine spirit are to join with community members working with phytoremediation plants to detoxify unhealthy lands; to inspire local farmers to organically rebuild and regenerate the soil; to plant beautiful flowers that we and the honeybees, birds, and butterflies will love.

As we nourish our inner life and help our outer environments thrive, we create the world we long for.

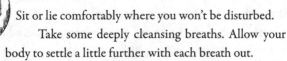

Practice

Sit or lie comfortably where you won't be disturbed.

Take some deeply cleansing breaths. Allow your body to settle a little further with each breath out.

Then, envision the lupine. Imagine the spray of starry leaflets at its base and the delicate blue-violet petals on the stalk of this beautiful plant. See, feel, sense, or intuit this nature being as clearly as you can. Feel its generous and luminous spirit.

Just as the Nootka lupine plant transmutes environmental toxins, feel your ability to transform. The alchemical power that is so natural to lupine is also natural to you. Take your time as you sense the radiance and love of this gentle being spontaneously transmute what is tangled inside of you.

You may notice a part of your body calling to you. Rest your palms there. Ask Lupine to help you sink deeply, as if with a taproot, into a secret earthly space where gifts are stored away like dried food before the winter. No chaos on the Earth's surface can penetrate this protected space.

Take your time. Drink in the silence and peace from this hidden place that sustains, nourishes, and transforms you.

Keep resting and settling more deeply into this interior space with each breath in and out as you continue to merge with Nootka Lupine. Allow the intelligence of this plant spirit to be one with you. Sense its strong and caring heart. Feel this heart-field radiate love and comfort within and all around you. Feel that this inner landscape is held by the Earth herself. Keep focusing on the abundance you feel inside.

You may become aware of compassionate forces or symbols. No matter your situation, feel the heart-wisdom and the power stored away for you to use, eat, and live on.

In whatever way feels right, gently transition from this practice when you feel ready. Sense the Lupine spirit with you. Feel rooted in the earth. Know that the inner pathways you illumine shine the light for others who are lost or suffering. When we become one with the web of life, we can convey radiance, love, and harmony to the collective. Use this time to reflect on concrete ways to share the wealth you have retrieved and to offer the richness out.

Nootka Lupine produces the loveliest blue-violet flowers, and they always make me smile. I use a lot of flowers in healing methods I learned from Quechua people in the high Andes. My Quechua friends say the beauty of the flowers and their sweet scents draw good spirits to the person.

After you have enacted the transmutational practice above, or any time you feel the need or desire, invite the renewing energy of sweet flower spirits.

Try taking a bath with flower petals floating in the water. Light a candle and play your favorite music as you invite the sweet spirits to cleanse you on the inside, brightening your life force. You will feel nourished.

You can also simply imagine lying in a bed of flowers or feeling flowers all around you. Sense as vividly as you can that flowers rest lightly all over your body, are strewn in your hair, and are tucked above your ears and gathered in the crooks of your elbows. A smile will come to your face. This is a sign that the sweet fragrances of the flower spirits are attracting good energies to you. The Quechua tell us that our happy hearts draw and radiate even more goodness.

Keep imagining as vividly as you can the beauty as well as the scents of your favorite flowers. You will feel brilliance and peace.

No matter our burdens, the healing balm is to live life fully, to shine our light, and to offer some good to the world.

In doing what stirs our heart and in being all we came here to be, we blossom like the pure spirit of beautiful lupine flowers that enrich the space for others.

Offering beauty and nourishment is a natural generosity that gives us purpose and strength.

The starry leaflets of the Nootka lupine that fan out in all directions remind us that all life on Earth is inherently cosmic. The humble spirit of the Lupine is a reminder of our starry origins and our ability to manifest our divine presence here on Earth. The promise of this era of light is to consciously integrate our cosmic and earthly aspects.

When we ponder our vast universe, it's easy to sense how precious and rare this human life is. None of us ever knows how long we will have on Earth. Like Nootka Lupine, which doesn't budge once it extends its taproot, may we hold to our highest visions for life. Just as lupine—through its short, delicate life—emanates beauty and enriches its environment, let us nurture goodness and harmony for all life and the Earth.

Closing Words to Inspire You

Sandra

For some, the journey through the Dark Night of the Soul can be quite intense. But it is also beautiful, conjuring amazing images even through the obscurity of the darkness. Nature comes to help, allies materialize and offer support, and though this process means traveling to some of the deepest, darkest places in your soul, we can take comfort knowing that no matter which path we decide to follow, we will find solutions.

Your spirit wakes up on such a journey. You pushed through the obstacles, the traumas, the past actions, the atrocities of the past, the illnesses you're dealing with now. You kept moving despite everything happening in the world, and you did not sit down in the dark.

So many of you died to the life you were living. Again, the point of an initiation is to die to an old way of life while you are still alive. Once you step back into the light of life, you still have an ego. You continue to hold certain feelings about life and what is happening in the world. But you can observe and just be with what comes up for you. After the journey, you will begin to understand that you are now more independent and grounded, and have a stronger sense of self. You don't require so much help from others to get through challenges in life. You do have the strength of spirit to carry you through any challenge life brings for you.

Basically, in every Dark Night of the Soul, you must rely on your spirit to be strong enough to deal with the angst, the panic, the fear, the anger that comes from being a human in the world today. It's a lot. But after reading this book, you will have the tools you need to walk through the darkness, should it become a part of your journey. And if you have been through the Dark Night of the Soul already, hopefully this book helped to put some of your experience into perspective.

The journey I took you on helped me walk through a very dark seven years of my life. I created a road map and collected tools that I used to get me through the obstacles. They helped me find light when it seemed nonexistent.

If you have ever struggled, may this book help you by giving you a different perspective on what you went through. Or, if you are traveling now, I hope it will support you. Nature and life are filled with beauty but also with obstacles to growth.

Have courage and keep moving forward, and eventually you will find yourselves stepping into the "light of the shaman." In this dimension of reality, you live the work you practice, so by seeking this light, you, too, can become a presence of healing in the world.

Llyn

I have found through my own journeys that although we each ultimately walk alone and the path can feel incredibly foreboding, wakeful presences are ever by our side. In my darkest hours, I reach out to invisible forces such as those Sandra and I have introduced you to in this book. When there is nothing to hold on to, these allies can help us revive our instinctual wisdom and remember the ever-present goodness that is part of life's deep mystery.

As our soul journey deepens, we find the gap between light and dark is softened. Life's joys and sorrows and those parts of us at odds with each other discover they can create a rich and resilient home together. As we each come home to ourselves in these ways, it helps heal separations that cause so much pain in the world. May the teachings in this book help you walk wakefully as you find your way back home.

Acknowledgments

Sandra

I am very grateful to Llyn Roberts for inviting me to write this much-needed book with her. It was a beautiful journey to watch as we supported each other through whatever each of us was dealing with during our time of writing. This has been an exciting project that we have both been so passionate about.

Eben Herrick did a magnificent job on his illustrations, and I am grateful to have gotten to know him. I felt his images bring a sweetness as well as power and magic to our book.

Jacirendi Xakhar came to my rescue in her copyediting help, as grammar is not my forte. I loved working with her. She is wise beyond her years and has such an expanded knowledge of life that she was able to share important feedback, inspiring me to dive a little deeper into my inner landscape to bring out the true wisdom I was trying to share. And she could point out how to make certain teachings more accessible to readers. I felt graced by her help.

I thank Barbara Moulton for her endless patience with us and her support of me as a friend and of my work for more than thirty years.

And it has been an exciting new adventure to work with Kate Zimmermann and her team at Union Square. Thank you for believing in us and for your exceptional guidance and support.

And I always want to acknowledge my husband, Woods. His support is everything to me.

I honor the nature beings that helped me learn about the path through the darkness and how it leads back to the light of life.

Llyn

It was such a delight to work with Sandra Ingerman. The understanding we conveyed to one another through the course of this creation supported me to dive deeply into the material and to share in an authentic way. It has been a powerful journey. I am grateful to Sandra for working together to offer this needed and inspired guidance.

I love the exquisite drawings in this book that were rendered by my son, Eben Herrick. The illustrations are meaningful and make the nature beings topics that Sandra and I write about come to life. I am also grateful to Eben for his extremely helpful feedback on my chapters.

My dear friends Caryn Markson, Alejandro Cordova, and Barbara Vane were so generous with their insights and encouragement as I lived through the materials presented here. I so appreciate their care as well as their resonance with the teachings in this book.

I am grateful to our literary agent, Barbara Moulton, for her gentle and astute guidance. Barbara has been wonderful in every way and has been a steady and positive presence through the publishing.

I have enjoyed working with our editor, Kate Zimmermann, whose skillful, sensitive work enhances the clarity of these writings. The team at Union Square is a pleasure to work with.

I honor my second- and third-year apprentices for their transformative work with allies such as those Sandra and I present—as they walk through darkness to embrace the creative spirit of life.

I extend my deepest gratitude to the indigenous elders and spiritual guides whose wisdom appears in this book. Their teachings to heal ourselves as we heal our relationship with the Earth is a profound and timely gift.

About the Authors

Sandra Ingerman, MA, a world-renowned teacher of shamanism, is recognized for bridging ancient cross-cultural healing methods with modern culture. She's taught for forty years, including worldwide workshops on shamanic journeying, healing, and reversing environmental pollution using spiritual methods.

Sandra is a licensed marriage and family therapist, professional mental health counselor, and a board-certified expert on traumatic stress. *Watkins Mind Body Spirit* magazine honored her by including her in their 100 Most Spiritually Influential People of 2020. She was also chosen as one of the Top 10 Spiritual Leaders of 2013 by *Spirituality and Health* magazine and was awarded the 2007 Peace Award from the Global Foundation for Integrative Medicine.

She's authored twelve books, including *Soul Retrieval: Mending the Fragmented Self*; *Medicine for the Earth*; *Walking in Light*; and *The Book of Ceremony: Shamanic Wisdom for Invoking the Sacred in Everyday Life*. Sandra and Hank Wesselman's book, *Awakening to the Spirit World: The Shamanic Path of Direct Revelation*, won both the 2011 COVR (Coalition of Visionary Resources) Visionary Award and the 2011 IPPY (Independent Publisher Book Award).

Since the 1980s, thousands of people have healed from past and present traumas through Soul Retrieval, the classic cross-cultural shamanic healing method Sandra teaches.

Sandra is recognized for bridging ancient cross-cultural healing methods into our modern culture, addressing the needs of our times.

Sandra is known for gathering the global spiritual community together to perform powerful transformative ceremonies as well as inspiring us to stand strong in unity so we do our own spiritual and social activism work while keeping a vision of hope and being a light in the world.

She is passionate about helping people to reconnect with nature.

Sandra joined in partnership with Renee Baribeau to create a weekly, thirty-minute podcast called *The Shamans Cave*.

Read more about Sandra online at:

sandraingerman.com

shamanicteachers.com

ShamansTV.com

Llyn "Cedar " Roberts, MA, is an award-winning author and a celebrated teacher of healing and shamanism. She teaches experiential programs that heal us and our relationship with the natural living world.

Her work incorporates her background in contemplative psychotherapy, Tibetan Buddhism, work in remote locations with diverse indigenous shamanic groups, East and West body-mind approaches to healing, and extended time in wilderness locations.

Her books include the 2015 Gold Nautilus Award–winning *Speaking with Nature* (coauthored with Sandra Ingerman), the 2012 Independent Publishers Award–winning book *Shapeshifting into Higher Consciousness*, *Shamanic Reiki* (coauthored with Robert Levy), and *The Good Remembering*.

She studied at the School for International Training in the early 1980s and completed an internship in India. In 1985, she received a Master of Arts degree in Tibetan Buddhist and Western Psychology from Naropa University. She was a psychotherapy intern at a Mexican American community mental health center in Denver.

Working in the nonprofit sector since 1997, she is the former director of Dream Change, Inc., founded by John Perkins and dedicated to encouraging an earth-honoring consciousness. After cofacilitating eight trips with John to work with Amazonian and Andean indigenous people in Ecuador, she created study experiences for people to learn from Quechua healers in the high Andes of Ecuador and in Tuva, Siberia (the latter with Bill Pfeiffer). She created and cofacilitated transformational workshops with John Perkins for more than fifteen years at the Omega Institute and at other world-class venues.

Together with John Perkins, she was a consultant to the University of Massachusetts at Dartmouth Sustainability Initiative and the nonprofit Earth Train, dedicated to preserve indigenous culture and the rain forests of Panama.

She is a mentor for the Transformational Travel Council and a member of the Evolutionary Leaders Circle founded by Deepak Chopra and Barbara Marx Hubbard. She served as adjunct faculty for the Graduate Institute as well as Union Graduate School.

In 2012, she founded the Olympic Mountain EarthWisdom Circle (OMEC), dedicated to inspiring a sacred and responsible relationship with the earth and to preserving the wisdom ways of ancient peoples. OMEC incepts publications, films, and other projects that preserve the myths and stories, ceremonies, and textile arts of indigenous communities in Siberia, Guatemala, and the Pacific Northwest. OMEC also promotes land projects, wilderness immersions, and nature-based writing programs that support its mission. For more than fifteen years, Llyn has facilitated sacred journeys to Guatemala for people to learn from Maya spiritual guides and to support OMEC projects that honor the spiritual and cultural heritage of Maya peoples. To learn more about OMEC and its indigenous projects, visit: eomec.org.

Having facilitated programs to teach how to heal with nature's spiritual energy for more than thirty years, she is the founder of Shamanic Reiki Worldwide (SRW), which offers experiential and nature-based approaches to energy healing. These are taught in three-year master healer–teacher apprenticeship certification trainings, home-based study formats, and online trainings, as well as in-person programs taught at various locations including at the Omega Institute in Rhinebeck, New York, where Llyn has taught for almost twenty-five years. To learn more about SRW, please visit shamanicreikiworld wide.com.

Llyn, through her work, promotes an expanded paradigm of well-being that nourishes us on this human journey as it also deepens our sense of belonging with the Earth. You can find out more about Llyn and contact her at llynroberts.com.

About the Artist

Eben Herrick is an award-winning contemporary artist with a Bachelor of Fine Arts degree from the Massachusetts College of Art and Design. His work spans a wide range of mediums, including digital illustrations, oil painting, and public murals. Eben's unique style seamlessly blends realism with abstract elements, bringing a sense of mystery and depth to his work.

To view more of Eben's work, follow him on Instagram @ebenherrick or visit his website at ebenherrick.com.

Other Books and Lecture Programs by Sandra Ingerman

Books

Soul Retrieval: Mending the Fragmented Self (HarperOne, 1991).

Welcome Home: Following Your Soul's Journey Home (HarperOne, 1993).

A Fall to Grace (fiction) (Moon Tree Rising Productions, 1997).

Medicine for the Earth: How to Transform Personal and Environmental Toxins (Three Rivers Press, 2001).

Shamanic Journeying: A Beginner's Guide (Sounds True, 2004).

How to Heal Toxic Thoughts: Simple Tools for Personal Transformation (Sterling, 2007).

Awakening to the Spirit World: The Shamanic Path of Direct Revelation book and drumming CD (cowritten with Hank Wesselman, winner of the Independent Publishers Award in 2011 and a COVR award). (Sounds True, 2010).

The Shaman's Toolkit: Ancient Tools for Shaping the Life and World You Want to Live In (Weiser, 2010).

Walking in Light: The Everyday Empowerment of a Shamanic Life (Sounds True, 2014).

Speaking with Nature: Awakening to the Deep Wisdom of the Earth (cowritten with Llyn Roberts) (Inner Traditions, 2015).

The Hidden Worlds (fiction for young adults; coauthored with Katherine Wood) (Moon Books, 2018).

The Book of Ceremony: Shamanic Wisdom for Invoking the Sacred in Everyday Life (Sounds True, 2018).

Audio Programs

The Soul Retrieval Journey (Sounds True, 1997).

The Beginner's Guide to Shamanic Journeying (Sounds True, 2003).

Miracles for the Earth (Sounds True, 2004).

Shamanic Meditations: Guided Journeys for Insight, Vision, and Healing (Sounds True, 2010).

Soul Journeys: Music for Shamanic Practice (Sounds True, 2010).

Shamanic Visioning: Connecting with Spirit to Transform Your Inner and Outer Worlds (6-CD audio program) (Sounds True, 2013).

Shamanic Visioning Music: Taiko Drum Journeys (Sounds True, 2014).

The Spirit of Healing: Shamanic Journey Music (with Byron Metcalf) (Sounds True, 2015).

App

Healing Your Thoughts